More Life Lessons From And For My Girlfriends

Shari Leid

Make Your Mess Your Message

More Life Lessons From And For My Girlfriends

Published by: Capucia, LLC
211 Pauline Drive #513
York, PA 17402

Paperback ISBN: 978-1-954920-11-8
eBook ISBN: 978-1-954920-12-5
Library of Congress Control Number: 2021914841

Cover Design: Zizi Iryaspraba Subiyarta / www.pagatana.com
Layout: Ranilo Cabo
Cover photo and author photos: Wendy K Yalom / www.Wendykyalom.com
Inside photos / black and whites: Natalie Wallace / www.nataliewallacephotography.com
Editor and Proofreader: Janis Hunt Johnson / www.askjanis.com
Book Midwife: Carrie Jareed

Printed in the United States of America

Make Your Mess Your Message

More Life Lessons From
And For My Girlfriends

This book is dedicated to my family: my supportive and good-looking husband Rory, my beautiful and creative daughter Alexis, and my extremely handsome and witty son Zachary — who have supported me as I embarked on a writing career after the age of fifty, writing my first book *The 50/50 Friendship Flow: Life Lessons From and For My Girlfriends* — and now on to my second book, with a third in the works. I am always feeling their love and support as I grow, learn, and find the messages in life's messes.

Preface

The Photo Shoot

In a book titled *Make Your Mess Your Message,* it simply makes sense that part of the process to complete the book was to tackle the mess of figuring out how to photograph fifty-one women during the COVID-19 pandemic — a mess that required a strict social-distancing protocol. I am thankful that photographer Natalie Wallace was willing to take on this challenging shoot.

Rather than working in the beautiful professional studio of Natalie Wallace Photography with its high ceilings and perfect lighting, we set up and shot from my living room couch via Zoom, which we streamed onto my large television screen. While researching how best to accomplish this task, we found that most of the Zoom-type shoots were being done with the subject physically at a professional studio or with a professional set-up, which included controlled lighting and high-definition cameras — not the usual mobile devices and laptops that our subjects were using. In addition to shooting from personal laptops and cell phone cameras, each subject was required to set up her own lighting and background space. These limitations made it impossible to achieve consistent clear, crisp, and uniform shots, not to mention that we had the additional layer of my television screen, through which we were shooting. While it was messy, we all showed up and embraced the challenge!

In addition to the screen challenges, we experienced poor internet connections that caused pixilation, poor lighting that caused shadows, and fifty-one different backgrounds. While most of the women shot from places located inside their homes, some shot from work, from outside, or even from a hotel corridor.

It was truly a mess-to-message experience: All fifty-one women showed up, we laughed, and we made our mess our message. We learned that we did not need to be perfect. The perfection was simply that all of us showed up. We showed up from Germany; Canada; Florida; Colorado; California; Virginia; Pennsylvania; Washington, D.C.; Alabama; and Washington state. We laughed at the mess throughout the two days of shooting. It is liberating to know that we can be imperfectly perfect, finding joy in the mess!

Again, special thanks to Natalie Wallace Photography for journeying through the mess with me.

"I don't know what's messier,
my hair or my life."
— Anonymous

Contents

Foreword		1
Author's Note		7
The Challenge		9
Chapter 1	Sarah Elizabeth's Story: Returning to Joy	15
Chapter 2	Tina's Story: Finding Strength in a Storm	21
Chapter 3	Kelli's Story: Going with the Flow	27
Chapter 4	Angie's Story: Recognizing Each Day as a Gift	33
Chapter 5	Jennifer C.'s Story: Overcoming Imposter Syndrome	39
Chapter 6	Tawan's Story: Defining Self-Worth	45
Chapter 7	Leah's Story: Choosing How to Respond	51
Chapter 8	Alla's Story: Moving from Surviving to Thriving	57
Chapter 9	Jen's Story: Learning to Love Myself	63
Chapter 10	Sarah E.'s Story: Creating Community	69
Chapter 11	Paige's Story: Finding Grace	75
Chapter 12	Jane's Story: Rejecting Stereotypes	81

Chapter 13 Jiawen's Story: Defining My Own Expectations 87
Chapter 14 Melissa's Story: Filling My Own Cup 93
Chapter 15 Caron's Story: Taking Time to Grieve 99
Chapter 16 Jennifer's Story: Learning the Importance of Self-Care During a Pandemic 105
Chapter 17 Kathryn's Story: Realizing That We Can All Grow and Change 111
Chapter 18 Gage's Story: Becoming a Role Model 117
Chapter 19 Sarah R.'s Story: Challenging Myself 123
Chapter 20 Susan's Story: Finding the Silver Lining 129
Chapter 21 Linda's Story: Letting Go of the To-Do List 135
Chapter 22 Rose's Story: Taking on Life's Obstacles as They Come 141
Chapter 23 Maja's Story: Finding the Beauty — Even in the Darkness 147
Chapter 24 Tee-Ta's Story: Breaking Free from Judgment 153
Chapter 25 Shay's Story: Resetting My Life During the Mess 159
Chapter 26 Mari's Story: Trusting My Intuition 165
Chapter 27 Alex's Story: Making Lemonade Out of Lemons 171
Chapter 28 Teri's Story: Enhancing Wellness and Longevity through Functional Nutrition 177
Chapter 29 Cati's Story: Letting Go of the Mess 183

Chapter 30	Lilla's Story: Removing a Title Can Allow Room for Grace	189
Chapter 31	Shalonda's Story: Treating Everyone Like Family—A Lesson from My Mother	195
Chapter 32	Carrie's Story: Opening Myself Up to Opportunity	201
Chapter 33	Dee Dee's Story: Having Faith Gets Me Through the Storm	207
Chapter 34	Carolyn's Story: Finding My Voice	213
Chapter 35	Bunni's Story: Standing Up for Myself	219
Chapter 36	Sarah's Story: Honoring Messages I Received from My Parents	225
Chapter 37	Cindy's Story: Loving My Child Through His Struggle with Addiction	231
Chapter 38	Lennaea's Story: Breaking the Cycle of Abuse	237
Chapter 39	Tracy's Story: Letting What is Important to Me Guide Me	243
Chapter 40	Ronda's Story: Trusting That I Am Able	249
Chapter 41	Yolanda's Story: Escaping Credit-Card Debt	255
Chapter 42	Roxanne's Story: Becoming Comfortable with Physical Displays of Affection	261
Chapter 43	Stacey's Story: Finding Perspective in the Mess	267
Chapter 44	Angela's Story: Living with Anxiety	273

Chapter 45 Tracie's Story: Fighting for My Son's Life 279

Chapter 46 Kirsten's Story: Doing Something Every Day That Scares Me 285

Chapter 47 Theresa's Story: Navigating Young Adulthood Without Parents to Guide Me 291

Chapter 48 Simone's Story: Growing Up Different 297

Chapter 49 Tiffani's Story: Acknowledging My Adoption Trauma 303

Chapter 50 Rachel's Story: Knowing I Can Get Through Any Mess 309

Chapter 51 Connie's Story: Accepting that I'm Imperfectly Perfect 315

Chapter 52 Author's Story: Sharing My Own Mess-to-Message Experience 321

Going Forward 331

Contact Us 333

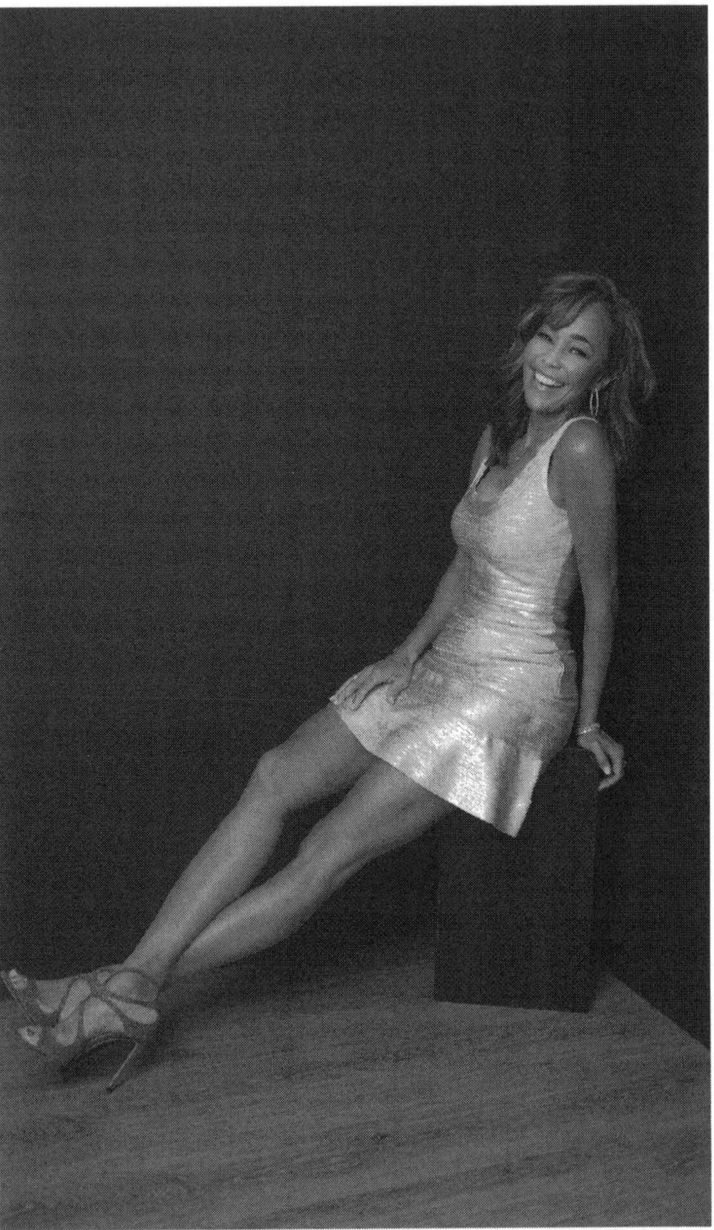

Foreword

I keep these words written by Swiss-American psychiatrist Elisabeth Kübler-Ross tacked to my refrigerator: *"The most beautiful people are those who have known defeat, known suffering, known struggle, known loss and have found their way out of the depths. These persons have an appreciation, a sensitivity, and an understanding of life that fills them with compassion, gentleness, and a deep loving concern. Beautiful people do not just happen."*

This quote reminds me of all of the beautiful people in my life, including my friend Shari Leid. Shari has known struggle, loss, and suffering. Her ability to be transparent, making her mess her message, is a genuine gift to all who are fortunate enough to know her. Shari's life is a testament to the strength of human resilience.

Shari's personal life messes aren't immediately apparent. From the exterior you see a beautiful, fit, world-traveled, petite, educated, talented wife — mother, daughter, and friend to many. Her home is warm and inviting and she hosts epic parties — including her famous annual holiday cookie exchange, where nearly ninety women from different ages, races, and backgrounds dress in that year's themed holiday festive attire and exchange a combined total of 5,400 cookies. The first year I attended, we all dressed as holiday elves. According to Shari, "When we are all wearing these silly and fun holiday costumes, it takes the focus away from our differences, and it simply makes it easier to engage with new friends who are outside of our regular circle of friends, in a fun holiday atmosphere." The exchange is much more than satiating our sweet tooth. Shari uses it as a platform for connecting the beautiful women in her life.

She is a former fitness trainer, former deputy prosecuting attorney, and former civil litigator. Shari rises early to wear all the hats that her full plate encompasses, which now includes author and life coach. However, the gift of Shari is that she doesn't leave others envious of her full life, talents, and blessings. She shares her journey and doesn't hide her messes that have become her messages. Some of that "mess" includes being adopted after being abandoned as an infant in Seoul, Korea; a double hip replacement; a breast cancer diagnosis; raising children very close in age; and now at middle age navigating marriage and an elderly parent.

Shari shares through her coaching, books, social media, and networking that you can indeed take your mess and make it your message. She also demonstrates courage and a wicked sense of humor, which I witnessed as she took to the stage at a theatre located behind the iconic Seattle Gum Wall in the landmark Pike Place Market to perform her first — and what she swears will be her only — stand-up comedy routine.

I, like all of the women in this book, have dealt with messes in my life — which for me includes my parents' divorce, my own divorce after twenty-four years of marriage, my children's father's untimely death, the death of my stepdaughter, taking care of a dying parent, and the pain that comes with family members and loved ones who suffer through drug and alcohol addiction. In my professional life, as a self-employed, single, African-American housing provider and entrepreneur, I have persevered through financial challenges, including surviving the downturn of 2007–2009 and now navigating the financial mess of the COVID-19 pandemic.

Through these life messes, as Shari has modeled the bravery in publicly sharing, is that our mess doesn't need to define or destroy us. We have the power to turn our messes into our messages. The stories in this book — which includes my sister Tracie's personal journey of having a son born with a rare congenital heart disease and Heterotaxy Syndrome, detailed in her award-winning book, *Incompatible with Nature: Against the Odds: A Parent's Memoir of Congenital Heart Disease* — give us hope and the freedom to take control of our messes.

I've learned that no matter how great or small our messes may be, we *all* suffer. Having quality friendships to help carry the load makes it all bearable. In today's social media world, it is easy to portray a life filled with only bliss. It is courageous individuals who speak their truth, no matter how painful — and their courage allows others to relate and to see more clearly their own path out of the mess.

As I write this, we have just entered the new year of 2021. Last year, with the pandemic, we all encountered more hardships than we could have ever conceived. We saw friends and family die, watched marriages dissolve, and witnessed businesses that once thrived close. We need now, more than ever, tools for how we will rise and make the best messages out of our messes. Thank you and cheers to Shari Leid, for creating this platform whereby we can all learn from each other and prosper.

— Dana Frank, Managing Partner, TD Frank Family Properties; Board Member of the Museum of Pop Culture; Board Member and Community Volunteer for Treehouse, serving youth in foster care; Member of the International Women's Forum; Community activist; and Co-Blogger at www.menopausebarbees.com

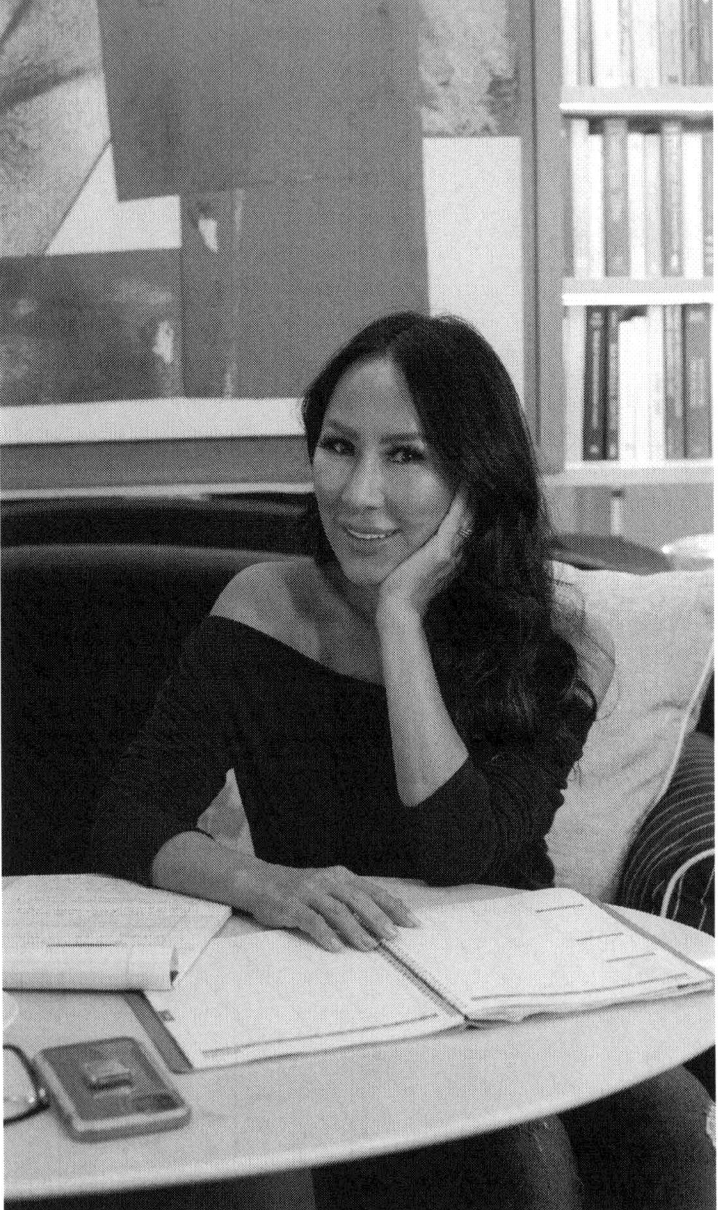

Author's Note

While we journey through life, with each twist and turn being uniquely our own, there are some human experiences that are universally true. One of these is that we all experience life's messes. Life is messy. Some messes roll off our backs like water on a duck, while others penetrate our soul. Over the course of spending time isolated from friends and family during the COVID-19 pandemic, I set a goal to speak with women from all walks of life, and to ask them the question: "What is the mess that became your message?" Not only did my relationships with each of the women I spoke to deepen, but I also learned that no matter the mess, there is always a message that can be found.

Join me, as I set out to ask my girlfriends, *What was the mess that became your message?*

The Challenge

This book is designed for you to read one chapter each week. You can do this alone, or grab a group of girlfriends to journey through the book together over the course of a year. Each week you'll have an opportunity to learn from a life mess that one of my girlfriends faced and to find out how she made her mess her message.

Following each chapter is a place to journal and an action step to take. Some of my girlfriends will remind you of your own girlfriends, and many of their messes will be messes that you've dealt with yourself or may have to handle in the future. Life is messy. Let's face it together.

My debut book, *The 50/50 Friendship Flow — Life Lessons From and For My Girlfriends,* challenged you to make a commitment to meet with five, ten, or even more of the girlfriends in your life — to let each friend know what she's brought to your life, your appreciation for her, and the lessons you've learned from her. This book's challenge has a slightly different spin.

Over the course of a year, commit to meet with at least three people, one on one:

1. **A life-long friend**
2. **A relative**
3. **A new acquaintance or someone you've known for a while but have never shared a meal with**

Let these individuals know that you have chosen to take the **Mess-to-Message Challenge.** Before your date, share the question you will be asking, so that they have the opportunity to really think about it ahead of time: **"What is the mess that became your message?"**

I guarantee that you will not just learn something about your friend or relative that you had not known before; it will also deepen your relationship, and you will become keenly aware of how connected we all really are.

Recognizing how messy all of our lives are and seeing the purpose in the mess gives us the perspective that allows us to live a life filled with choice, freedom, and opportunity.

For fun, take a photo and document your date on social media using the hashtag **#messtomessagechallenge**

Make *Your Mess Your Message* Challenge

Over the course of a year, commit to meet with at least three people, one on one:

1. A life-long friend
2. A relative
3. A new acquaintance or someone you've known for a while but have never shared a meal with

Ask the question, "What is the mess that became your message?"

#messtomessagechallenge

"What is the mess that
became your message?"
— Anonymous

Chapter 1

Sarah Elizabeth's Story: Returning to Joy

Born in El Paso, Texas

Fun fact: Sarah spoke Spanish before English, being raised in an exclusively Mexican life until she was four, when her family moved to Wisconsin and she had to learn English because no one spoke Spanish at her school.

Sarah and I met through a mutual friend who introduced us on Facebook nearly a decade ago. Through the years, Sarah and I attended many of the same events (often fashion shows), but we didn't know one another well enough to say much more than hello as we passed each other with our different groups of friends in tow. It wasn't until this past year that she and I made it a point to get together for happy hour at a restaurant located about halfway between where she and I live, and that's when we finally had a chance to sit down and really get to know one another. Our friendship easily took off from there. We both instantly recognized why our mutual friend thought we were meant to be friends. Our conversation flowed effortlessly.

Date 1 — What is the mess that became your message?

One of my favorite things about Sarah is that she doesn't shy away from talking about the hard stuff. I think of her as a realist — someone who sees the world and situations for what they are — not letting herself get pulled far down a rabbit hole of drama, exaggeration, or frivolous matters. When I asked her if she'd talk to me for this project, I was thrilled when she agreed because I knew that whatever she decided to share would be open, honest, and told without fear of judgment.

Sarah shared a time in her very young adult life that helped shape who she is today. She started by telling me that at age seventeen, she was unable to attend the college that she had planned to attend because her dad was dying. As an only child and close to her dad, she needed and wanted to help care for him. Her dad was dying of AIDS, an illness that had more fear than knowledge around it at the time.

During that period, while in her freshman year of college, she was invited to a party by a high school friend who encouraged her to attend because he saw that she needed a break, that she needed to simply have some fun. Sarah knew he was right — and quite frankly, she wanted to go to the party and get drunk, to have a moment to forget about everything that was weighing so heavily on her. At the party, she ran into the boy she had dated throughout much of her high school years — reminding her of a time when life hadn't been messy. Sarah wanted to escape life for just that one night — a night to not worry about school, work, or her dad. And that one night of escape resulted in an unplanned pregnancy, which ultimately brought her beautiful daughter into the world.

Sarah used the word *crap* to define her 20s. She was from a small town, and her family was well-known in the town. As an unmarried teenage girl, she was judged for being pregnant. Before her daughter was born, her beloved father died. Sarah shared a heart-warming memory: Before her dad died, he wanted a hug and then asked her where she felt the hug. When she touched her heart, he said, "Yes, that is where I'll always be."

Even through her overwhelming grief, and as a single mom, she managed to finish college and work while raising a young daughter. Her mom, whom she is also close to, wasn't able to help her in the way she normally would have, because her mother was also going through her own profound period of grief. Sarah was on her own. She did marry during this time — not to her son's father, but to another man. Unfortunately, that marriage dissolved, which added even more trauma to the mess.

Sarah defines her 30s as a decade of *fight*. Even though she ended the volatile marriage, and her dad had passed several years earlier, she remained in that fight stage — just trying to survive. She didn't realize that she was stuck in this high-adrenaline phase until she began to experience panic attacks in her late thirties. The panic attacks were her wake-up call, as she realized that somewhere in the two decades of working to survive, she had lost herself.

The work continued for Sarah into her 40s. She realized that she needed to connect back to what she loved before the mess. She saw that she needed to take time to remember the person she was before life became something that she was always just reacting to, rather than really living. She wanted to find again what she had loved as a child.

For Sarah, the start of getting back to herself was to get back to church. She loved attending church as a child but rejected organized religion during her early adulthood, feeling betrayed by God. She wanted to get back to that sense of peace that she'd felt from attending church services as a child. She was able to find a church that she related to, and started attending services, getting back to who she was before the mess.

Sarah realized that with all that she had accomplished in her 30s, it was done from "a place of fight"; but in her 40s she recognized that she could accomplish just as much, if not more, from "a place of joy, love, and stability" — which turned out to be much healthier for her soul.

The mess: A dad dying of AIDS, an unplanned teenage pregnancy, and a marriage ending — all in her 20s while working and finishing college — experiencing deep grief and raising a child, while still a child herself.

The message: Fight or flight is a survival response which is needed at times, but it's not a place to live in. If you're living in fight-or-flight mode, take a step back to find yourself. Remember who you were before the mess.

Action step: Think about the things that you loved to spend your time doing as a child.

Journal

Todays date is:

As a child, I loved to:

Chapter 2

Tina's Story: Finding Strength in a Storm

Born in Surrey, England

Fun fact: Tina loves the Tudor period of history, which inspired her to hold her wedding at Thornbury Castle, a small castle where Henry VIII stayed with Anne Boleyn.

I met Tina through a mutual friend. While we've both lost touch with that mutual friend, Tina and I have managed to stay in contact through social media and have been fortunate to attend a few social gatherings together. Tina's friendly nature shines through. She is one of the most thoughtful persons I've ever met. I'll never forget my wonderful holiday surprise, after we were just newly acquainted: I received a fruit cake from her that her parents brought over from England, after I'd posted on Facebook that I was the only one at my house who absolutely loves fruitcake.

Date 2 — What is the mess that became your message?

Imagine being a newlywed, moving to another country, and just a month later, 9/11 happens. Your life is instantly turned upside down.

Tina met and married her husband, a member of the US Air Force, while he was stationed in the UK. Not too long after they were married, they moved to the United States, stationed at Hurlburt Field Air Force Base in Mary Esther, Florida. It was August 2001. Tina didn't know a soul and was in the process of trying to establish financial credit in the United States, learning to drive on the wrong side of the road, and finding out about things that seem simple. For instance, she discovered that going through a drive-thru was nearly impossible, because communicating an order through the intercom was very difficult given her English accent.

It was the morning of September 11th, 2001, and she was waiting for her cable TV to be connected. The cable service person came to her door looking shaken. Realizing that because Tina didn't have her television set hooked up yet, so she didn't know what was happening, he quickly connected the cable, just in time for her to witness the second plane crash into the Twin Towers. Immediately, her heart sank. She knew she was going to lose her husband. He would be deployed.

And just as she had feared on the morning that she saw the horrific news, within a week after 9/11 her husband was deployed. A few days prior to his deployment, the squadron spouses were called on base and told that their spouse was going to Location X. They weren't allowed to know the location, and correspondence would be available only through the mail — with a 3- to 4-week delay. It was explained that phones might eventually be possible but that was not guaranteed.

And, to add to the mess of that week of deployment, her car engine died, and she had to quickly learn how to drive her husband's stick-shift truck so that she could take him to the base to drop him off. After dropping him off, not only was she alone, but she had to drive herself home — on what to her, living her entire life in England, was the wrong side of the street — and she was driving for the first time by herself in a stick-shift truck. I imagine that moment as she drove home, as symbolic of the next few months. While she knew how to drive, driving a stick shift was something very foreign and frightening. And there she was, alone in a country where the language is the same but the dialect and accent, among many other things, were different enough that it made her feel lost. Her life was definitely messy.

Within a month of moving to the United States, Tina was all alone in a foreign country without friends or family. While there was a lot of mess as she tried to navigate life on her own in the United States, Tina's message is that when you are thrown into a storm, you can learn how strong you really are. This includes gaining confidence in your own abilities and finding out how much you can accomplish on your own. She went on to get a job, meet new people, and get comfortable with driving on the wrong side of the road as she navigated life's inevitable messes.

The mess: Being uprooted and alone in a new country.

The message: When you are thrown into a storm, you find out how strong you really are.

Action step: Try something brand-new this week and notice how you feel while attempting or completing the new activity.

Journal

Todays date is:

My strengths have come out when Ive been thrown into a storm. My strengths are:

"Creativity is messy,
and I am very creative."
— Anonymous

Chapter 3

Kelli's Story: Going with the Flow

Born in Walla Walla, Washington

Fun fact: When first married, Kelli once collected owl pellets from her yard to sell to a biological supply company for education. While she made about $150 for a job that took her only a few minutes to do, her "profession" made for unusual conversation. Now, she is a co-owner of both a farm and a winery (www.kontoscellars.com) — two professions that are easier to describe at a dinner party than owl-pellet sales.

Kelli and I met through Kelli's cousin, my good friend, Vanessa. I love Kelli's candor, and her humor. I also admire the relationship she has with her husband and daughters. I have joked with my girlfriend Vanessa that she should not look to Kelli and her husband as role models for what a marriage should look like because they set an unreasonably high bar. I love that when you are with them, it feels like you're with newlyweds because of the way they lovingly interact with one another.

Date 3 — What is the mess that became your message?

There are some girlfriends we have, that when we think about spending time with them, we automatically start laughing. Kelli is one of those girlfriends. She has a way of making even the most miserable situations turn into something that can be laughed at. She certainly did not disappoint me on our Zoom date.

In fact, while she had a lovely glass of red wine with her during our date, even though I happened to be drinking tea, I found that I laughed as much as I would have had I been drinking wine alongside her.

Kelli had always assumed that "one of her flaws" was being a poor planner. She's not a list person, so when she decides she wants to do something, she often just goes for it, taking a leap of faith. Knowing this about herself, it is not surprising that when she thought about a mess in her life, the mess she thought of stemmed from a lack of plans.

Several years ago, when her children were still fairly young, Kelli and her husband found that they had to cancel a planned anniversary trip to New York City due to unplanned medical reasons. Fortunately, the medical problems sorted themselves out just prior to their anniversary, and they found that they were once again available to travel. Deciding that they wanted to make the trip a family trip rather than just a couple's trip, they scrambled to find out where they could go as a family for a last-minute vacation. They discovered that they could get from eastern Washington to the island of Kauai. And, just about sixteen hours after deciding they could travel to Kauai, they landed.

Once arriving in Kauai, they were shocked to learn that there were absolutely no cars available for them to rent. I have never been to Kauai, so Kelli described for me an island that is still rather remote with limited public transportation and taxis. (This was long before the popular Uber and Lyft rideshare apps became available).

On a taxi ride to the resort, while trying to figure out what they were going to do, and speaking with their cab driver about their predicament, they drove past a moving-truck rental business. The thought arose, "Could we just rent a U-Haul?"

After arriving at the resort and spending a day learning that they were limited in what they could do — with very little within a reasonable walking distance, especially with two young children in tow — they decided to call the truck-rental business. Soon Kelli's husband had set off to rent a moving truck. While envisioning that perhaps it would not be so bad to have a small truck to take them around the island, her husband arrived back at the resort with the one truck the business had available: a full-sized moving truck!

This is how they spent their week on the island — traveling from place to place in a full-sized moving truck, equipped with back-up loud beeping warning sounds that couldn't be turned off. Their cute boutique resort had only valet parking available. The valet attendants graciously found a spot for the truck — which was too high to fit into their parking structure.

Kelli had a big smile on her face as she recalled how kind the people of Kauai were on that trip. She found the local community to be much more welcoming than what they may have experienced as regular tourists. Because they had the U-Haul truck, everyone assumed they were locals, so they were treated and embraced as such. Their rental for the week? Just over $100 — vs. the $200/day that a rental car vehicle would have cost. They had an adventure in paradise that reminds me of the best comedy movies.

Kelli realized that while she used to think that being a poor planner was one of her flaws, it has actually been one of her blessings — always resulting in some of the most fun memories she and her family have ever experienced.

Kelli challenged *me* to go on vacation without a plan. I told her I would have to figure out how to plan to be unplanned! But, after hearing the fun memories and adventures that can happen when you simply let life happen, I just may muster up the courage to take her up on the challenge.

The mess: The need to pivot and improvise because of lack of solid planning.

The message: Often the best and most memorable times in life stem from the unplanned moments.

Action step: Block off a day — a free day in which you have no plans. Simply wake up and find out where the day takes you!

Journal

Todays date is:

Im going to take a leap of faith this week. Im not sure how or when, but when the opportunity arrives, Im simply going to jump in! The thought of being spontaneous makes me feel:

Chapter 4

Angie's Story: Recognizing Each Day as a Gift

Born in Manila, Philippines
Fun fact: Angie always eats M&Ms in order by color: brown, orange, yellow, green, and last but not least, red.

Angie appears much younger than her nearly sixty years of age. She has a ready smile but can easily dive into a very serious and somber conversation. She is always ready to put her problem-solver hat on when needed. As I'm only 5'2" tall, I appreciate the fact that Angie is one of the only friends I have who is actually noticeably shorter than I am. However, don't let her petite frame fool you. She carries herself like she is six feet tall — never one to back down from sharing her truth or stepping up when help is needed.

Angie and I met through our husbands. Rob, Angie's first husband, worked in the Special Investigation Unit of a large insurance company, a company which is a client of my husband, an attorney practicing in the area of insurance defense. Both men became friends over the years, and one day my husband and I invited Angie's family over to our home for a barbeque. If I recall correctly, Rob was known for his slow-cooker baked beans, which he brought over to share.

Date 4 — What is the mess that became your message?

Eight years ago, Angie's world turned upside down. Rob died suddenly due to a ruptured brain aneurysm. He had been getting ready to take their only child to school. Their daughter, Gabby, was thirteen years old at the time, the apple of his eye. He was in the hospital for only a day. Three surgeries were performed, but he never regained consciousness. Angie waited to speak with Rob's brother before she agreed with the doctors to remove Rob from life support. Thankfully, Rob had a DNR (Do Not Resuscitate directive), which also helped guide Angie's gut-wrenching decision to remove him from life support. Both Angie and their young daughter were in the room when he passed. Angie still remembers her daughter's sobs as the most heartbreaking cry she has ever heard.

All of a sudden, Angie was a single mom. Her focus was to make sure that her daughter was okay. Suddenly losing Rob's salary, Angie was now fully responsible for making sure that she and her daughter were financially sound. She was running her own insurance agency at the time. She had clients to take care of. Everything fell on her.

Following Rob's death, Angie enrolled her daughter in group therapy. Angie explained to me that there are different groups that exist for children who lose parents, formed based on how the parent died. There were groups for kids who lost parents to long-term illness, and there were groups for kids who lost parents suddenly, as her daughter had. Part of the requirements for these groups was that the surviving parent also attend counseling. While counseling was not something Angie would typically gravitate towards, she made the decision to attend group counseling. During the counseling, in true Angie fashion, she recognized the heartache and tragedy of others around her, feeling empathy for those who seemed in her mind to be in worse places than she was. She focused on their problems rather than facing her own tragedy and loss.

It took her at least three years to recognize her own need to take care of herself. An anxiety attack, which mimicked symptoms of a heart attack, resulted in hospitalization. This was the moment she realized she needed to focus on her own healing.

Angie took an inventory of her life, and the following message came to her: Life is short. Learn to ask for help. Taking care of one's self is not selfish. Physical health must be made a priority, so learn the subtle art of *not giving a f#@k* about the small stuff.

Angie credits a book that she found, *This I Know: Notes on Unraveling the Heart* by Susannah Conway, for helping her immensely through the grief process. For Angie, the healing didn't begin at group counseling but instead was simply found in a book. Through the mess, she learned to be open and vulnerable. She realized that people, even her closest friends and family members, saw her as strong — but she didn't always need to be. Angie learned the power that comes from being okay with asking for help and finding time for self-care, even in the darkest of life's moments.

The mess: A family devastated by the sudden loss of a husband and father.

The message:

1. Life is short.
2. Ask for help.
3. Taking care of yourself is not selfish.
4. Physical health has to be a priority.
5. Learn the subtle art of *not giving a f#@k* about the small stuff.

Action step: Notice this week how many minutes you set aside for self-care — activities like exercise, reading a book, meditating, and journaling.

Journal

Todays date is:

This week, I am going to carve out an extra thirty minutes of time for the following self-care activity:

Chapter 5

Jennifer C.'s Story: Overcoming Imposter Syndrome

Born in Everett, Washington
Fun fact: Jennifer loves Elton John, so if you're riding in the car with her, she can belt out any of his songs on request.

I met Jennifer about ten years ago at a brunch. There were about a dozen women in attendance. Jennifer had been invited to the brunch through a mutual friend who knew that she would fit right in with the group of women who had come together that morning. Unfortunately, the table we were seated at was a long rectangular table, which made it difficult for us to communicate since she and I were seated several seats away from one another. So we didn't really say much more than "Nice to meet you." But as I've learned, it is often those brief meetings that can lead to the best friendships.

Social media was the stepping stone that took us from that brief weekend morning meeting to a friendship that allows us to text or call one another at the drop of a hat. We know that at any time of the day or night, we will carve out the time needed to listen and respond. We initially bonded as moms navigating the challenges of parenthood — and we formed a tighter bond as women navigating life's twists and turns.

Date 5 — What is the mess that became your message?

Jennifer spoke candidly with me during our Zoom date. She shared that the mess that became her message stemmed from her experience of living on her own, as a single mom, in New York City.

Jennifer resided in the Seattle area, working in the real estate industry. While in Seattle, she met and fell in love with a man from New York City. He happened to come from a very wealthy family, a family which was part of an upper social class that Jennifer was not raised in. While money wasn't the impetus for their dating or subsequent marriage, she certainly welcomed the security of not having to struggle alone. Jennifer had been a working single mom who not only had a young son and daughter, but she also had the additional challenge that her daughter was non-verbal at the time, with a diagnosis of autism at a very young age.

Her new husband wanted to live near his family in New York. Years prior to meeting him, Jennifer had read about The Rebecca School in New York City, arguably the best school and program in the country for children on the autism spectrum. Jennifer realized that in addition to sharing a life in New York City with her husband, she would now have the opportunity to enroll her daughter in a world-renowned school that would serve her daughter well.

Jennifer sold her home in Seattle and her car, and moved to New York City with her two young children. Soon after her move, however, her marriage crumbled. She was forced to figure out how to make ends meet, alone with her kids, in a city she did not know.

Jennifer had grown up poor and watched her parents lose their home. Her family was evicted when she was sixteen years old. That loss had sat with her. From the moment she moved to New York City, she felt that she was an imposter — as if she were living a fake life. She expected that the walls were going to come crashing in on her, just as they did for her family. Arguably, when her marriage crashed, her worst fears had come to fruition.

However, there was a message in the mess.

She made it on her own. Unbelievably, she was able to find an apartment for her and her two children that she could afford, located in an area of New York City that allowed her daughter to continue to attend The Rebecca School. She made her own real estate connections, and built her business from the ground up. She stayed in New York for four years — because her daughter was thriving and eventually became verbal. This was a miracle in and of itself.

Jennifer's struggle and triumph allowed her to realize that she can trust herself. She no longer feels like an imposter. She is confident in her abilities, knowing that she can handle whatever life brings her way.

She finally moved back to Seattle when an individual at The Rebecca School told Jennifer that she recognized how much Jennifer had sacrificed of herself by staying for four years on her own in New York. This woman assured her that her daughter could survive anywhere — and that it was okay to return home to Seattle.

Jennifer and her daughter soon moved back to Seattle. Her son had already returned there, so she was so thankful to be back with him on the West Coast. She returned as a mom who was not just barely surviving and waiting for the other shoe to drop, but actually thriving. She knew that no matter what, she was going to be okay.

The mess: Uprooting a life to move across the country for a relationship that quickly failed.

The message: I can survive on my own. I'm not an imposter who has to worry about my beautiful life disappearing in a second. I create my own good life out of whatever comes my way.

Action step: Celebrate something that you are proud of — something that you have created on your own.

Journal

Todays date is:

I remember the following life mess that I conquered on my own, which became my message:

Chapter 6

Tawan's Story: Defining Self-Worth

Born in Shreveport, Louisiana
Fun fact: Tawan's favorite song of all time is *Redemption Song* by Bob Marley.

Tawan and I met about twenty years ago. Her husband Brett and I practiced law in the same Tacoma, Washington law firm. Over the years, she and I have become good friends. As I've gotten to know Tawan, I'm impressed by her many talents and interests. She is a former college tennis athlete; a motorcyclist; a chef (and owner of Fo' Cheezie); a senior paralegal at the family law firm; and a former police sergeant, serving twenty years on the force. Tawan doesn't see obstacles as blockades; she looks at them as challenges to overcome.

Date 6 — What is the mess that became your message?

When I asked Tawan what her mess was that became her message, she immediately began speaking about her years in law enforcement. We happened to be having this conversation in the midst of the Black Lives Matter and Blue Lives Matter movements following George Floyd's death. As a Black woman, a mom to a Black son, and a former career law-enforcement officer, both movements weighed heavily on her heart. Having this discussion during such a hard time gave me an even deeper level of admiration for Tawan's strength and perseverance. It was apparent by her body language that the civil unrest occurring across our country had taken an emotional toll on her.

Tawan went into law enforcement because she wanted to help people. She recalls that from a very young age, she felt that she had the drive to do good in the world. She was incredibly proud when she graduated from the law enforcement academy. She was thrilled to be serving the community as a first responder. During her academy days, she became close to her classmates and strong bonds were formed. She assumed similar bonds would be formed in the department that she joined.

Unfortunately, her experience was anything but the support and encouragement that she had experienced in the academy. She was challenged with sexism and racism throughout her long career in law enforcement. Tawan expected a certain level of bad behavior towards her on the street, but the sexist and racist behavior also came from members of her own department. On the street, she would often notice that witnesses and victims of crime would choose to talk only to her less-experienced White counterparts; and on more than one occasion she had racial slurs thrown her way.

In her department, she received the subtle and often not-so-subtle message that she was never going to advance as high as she desired. She was forced to jump through hoops that many of her White male counterparts did not have to jump through. She was given less-desirable work shifts and denied training opportunities. She watched less-qualified co-workers be promoted ahead of her. This made her daily job more difficult than it already was. There were days when she would sit in her car in the parking lot and have to gather her mental strength, to remind herself why she chose to enter into a career in law enforcement in the first place, before she could walk back into that hostile work environment.

Tawan had to dig deep to find her own identity. During her two decades on the force, even with her years of experience she often got the shifts no one wanted — the swing shift or the night shift. She realized that her confidence had to come from within and not be based on the way she was treated, nor on others' attempts to chip away at her self-worth.

In the mess, she found her power. She found herself. She found her identity from within. She had been told *no* so many times during her years in law enforcement, eventually her reaction turned from being upset to a laugh — with the knowledge that she was committed to succeed despite the obstacles that were placed in front of her.

The mess: A work environment that is toxic — facing racism, sexism, and sexual harassment — in a profession where you're not welcome.

The message: Others can't define your worth no matter how hard they try. Your self-worth comes from within.

Action step: During the upcoming week, notice where your feelings of self-worth are coming from. Are your feelings of self-worth based upon what happens on social media? Are you counting on the reactions of others to feel good about yourself? Or do you base your self-worth on a confidence you carry within you?

Journal

Todays date is:

My self-worth can only come from me. I know Im worthy because:

Chapter 7

Leah's Story: Choosing How to Respond

Born in Tallmadge, Ohio
Fun fact: Leah grew up in a full house, the second of eight siblings.

Leah and I met through a mutual girlfriend who invited Leah to a small girls' night out gathering. We immediately hit it off and found that we have many mutual friends. In fact, Leah and I have more contact with each other now than we do with the girlfriend who initially brought us together.

Date 7 — What is the mess that became your message?

Leah has suffered with New Daily Persistent Headache (NDPH) for thirteen years. The name of the disorder is misleading. While every day is a new day, the headache is not new. Leah has had this same headache since August 7, 2007. I was not familiar with the disorder and was very interested to learn more about it — not only from speaking with Leah but also from reading about it on my own. I found out that one of the remarkable facts about the disorder is that most people who suffer from it can remember the exact day the headache began. Some days are better than others, but every day there is a headache. There are days when the headache is absolutely disabling.

The first three years of living with NDPH were the hardest for Leah. Both she and her husband at the time were self-employed and did not have medical insurance, so all of her procedures were paid for out of pocket. Bills ran into the thousands during the lengthy diagnostic phase. Because so little is known about the cause of NDPH, the diagnostic process can be quite lengthy and uncertain. For Leah, this phase included a possible misdiagnosis of an essentially inoperable physical cause that amounted to a death sentence.

After receiving conflicting medical opinions, Leah is still left with an unclear cause of her NDPH. The headache, mounting medical bills, and inconclusive diagnoses sent Leah into an emotional spiral. She hit her low about five years into the disorder. Leah shared with me that before her own experience, it had always been hard for her to understand how anyone could think of suicide, when they had children and a family to take care of and to love them. But after her experience she now understands the despair that people can fall into — a despair so profound that it causes the false belief that the ones they love would be better off without them.

One of the most pivotal moments for Leah happened when she was sitting in a neurosurgeon's waiting room and an elderly woman whom she did not know looked directly into her eyes and said three words: "Engage your faith." Those three simple words pierced her deeply. They were the catalyst for healing — not from the NDPH itself but from the emotional toll that it had taken on her life. Leah began to take back her power.

One of the things that Leah has done since taking back her power is that she acknowledges the headache on her headache anniversary. She looks at it as a day of reflection — a day to look back on the year and renew her goals. She has decided that while the headache has taken much from her, it hasn't taken away her ability to choose how to respond nor her ability to have control of her life.

Leah told me that the message from her mess is to have faith, and to live each day to the fullest as if you were dying. She has learned that she is more resilient than she ever knew was possible.

The mess: A headache that has been around for over thirteen years, which is sometimes utterly immobilizing.

The message:

1. Have faith in God that you will never be given more than you can handle, and that there is a purpose in your suffering.
2. Live each day like it is your last.
3. You are more resilient than you'll ever even know.

Action step: The three words that Leah needed to hear were *engage your faith.* What three words do you need to hear right now, and what meaning will they bring for you going forward?

Journal

Todays date is:

The three words that I am going to carry with me this week as my mantra are:

"Nothing is work unless
you'd rather be doing
something else."
— Anonymous

Chapter 8

Alla's Story: Moving from Surviving to Thriving

Born in Tashkent, Uzbekistan

Fun fact: Alla directed and acted in a play seen by hundreds of people, including diplomats, at the tender age of twenty.

Alla and I met a few years ago when we trained together to become life coaches. We worked and learned together for a good year. Due to the nature of the training, we got to know one another quickly — often sharing raw parts of our lives through the exercises in class and subsequent out-of-class practice coaching hours that our training required.

Date 8 — What is the mess that became your message?

Alla was born in Uzbekistan. She witnessed her country, which was then part of the Soviet Union, collapsing when she was just twelve years of age. Upon reflection, she says this was probably the time that she began living her life in survival mode, seeking out challenges instead of pleasures, and having fears based upon learning early on that life isn't always safe. She became afraid to embrace peace and fun, because both stopped feeling natural.

At age fifteen, she was the recipient of The Freedom Support Act, which was a United States–funded program. It allowed her to study abroad in America, something very rare for children from Uzbekistan, especially in the early 1990s. When she returned home at age sixteen, she finished school and then began working. She became the breadwinner of her family of four, working as a translator. This caused great pressure for her. Still a child herself — knowing that she had the most income potential in her family because of her language skills — she not only felt the heavy pressure of supporting her family but also felt stuck in a job and in a country that offered very little opportunity for advancement.

While in her late teens and early 20s, she continuously thought, "How am I going to get out of Uzbekistan?" Her family was very poor, and the country's economy was failing. It took six years for Alla to immigrate to the US. At age twenty-three, without any friends or family there, she emigrated to America. Alla is grateful for her parents' acquaintances who were already in the US; she had never met them before, but they were a point of help for her and are now like family. One day, shortly after arriving in the US, she noticed that for the first time since she was seventeen, her mind was quiet. She recognized that for the first time in years, her mind was not consumed with her need to find an escape.

She met a man in the US, married, and had two beautiful daughters. Unfortunately, during the last few years of their seventeen-year marriage, she could see that it was not the right marriage for her. Again she found herself as the family breadwinner, financially supporting her husband and children. She started to feel the same feelings she had encountered when she was trying to figure out how to leave Uzbekistan. She felt the pressure of financially supporting her family in a marriage that was not thriving — and once again she felt trapped.

Alla became consumed with how she again could *escape*. Finally, she found the courage to get a divorce and start over. She saw that she needed to learn who she was as a woman now in her 40s. She wanted to figure out if the expectations that she had always had for herself were real or imagined. Throughout her life up to that point, she had always done everything out of the need to survive as opposed to focusing on what she needed to thrive.

She realized that she didn't have to continue to hold onto the fears and traumas inspired by the past or to continue to be caught up in depleting situations. She began to embrace what she had learned as a teen and young adult. In doing so she became open to joy, love, and the world around her. As she continued on her journey of self-discovery, Alla recognized that once she started to experience the freedom to live a life filled with fun and choice, it became "a natural force" that grew and grew.

She shared with me a quote from Russian writer Mikhail Bulgakov that she loves, which describes this feeling:

"Well, as everyone knows, once witchcraft gets started, there's no stopping it."

The mess: Being stuck and living in survival mode.

The message: Give yourself permission to let go of the traumas of the past, which will then allow you to move from simply surviving to actually thriving.

Action step: Take an honest look at who you are today and recognize the incredible growth that you have achieved in spite of past traumas.

Journal

Today's date is:

Today, I'm going to let go of past traumas, which will allow me to see the blessings and opportunities that I can be grateful for right now today, and every day in the future. I will list my blessings here each day this week:

Chapter 9

Jen's Story: Learning to Love Myself

Born in Phoenix, Arizona
Fun fact: Jen once appeared on the popular 1970s television show, *Romper Room*.

Jen and I met in the early 1990s when I took a Spring Break trip during law school to visit my undergrad college roommate, Melissa, who was residing in the Pasadena area of California (*see Chapter 14*). Jen was working at the college where Melissa's father was serving as president. I instantly liked Jen. She was kind and funny, with an energy that makes people around her feel good. I remember on that visit that I had fun trying new things — like getting on stage at a karaoke bar with a group of women, which included Jen. Being tone deaf, I'm pretty sure I lip-synched our group song, for the sake of the audience's ears. Jen and I would go on to see each other through the years, and we were both bridesmaids at Melissa's wedding.

Date 9 — What is the mess that became your message?

The mess for Jen is something that built up over time. It manifested as a diagnosis of Chronic Hidden Hyperventilation coupled with significant weight problems. The health problems were a symptom of the choices that Jennifer had been making in her life, many to fill the void she felt because of her internal struggle for acceptance.

Jen, like me, was adopted. She comes from a family of three children, she and her younger brother being adopted. Her sister (who is the oldest of the three) and her mother have always had an easy relationship, but Jen often felt that her relationship with her mom suffered in comparison.

Looking back, she realizes that from a young age, she always tried to be perfect to obtain love and acceptance. The striving for perfection and the desire to achieve acceptance led Jen to attempt perfection in every area of her life. She tried to be a perfect daughter, friend, student, employee — yet she was putting her energy into everything but herself. An example from the most recent years can be found in her work. She would allow her vacation days at her job to build and build, never taking time off for herself to enjoy a vacation. She was living a life of high stress and anxiety — a life that stemmed from equating perfection with validation.

Through the process of dealing with her health challenge, she recognized that she was putting her energy into everything but herself. Through self-discovery, at the time of our virtual meeting, Jen had managed to lose over seventy pounds, nearing her goal weight.

Both her internal and external transformation has brought her so much joy that she has made it her mission to help others who are struggling with weight — a passion that has led her to becoming an incredibly successful, passionate, and knowledgeable health coach. She helps her clients not only to lose weight but even more importantly to recognize the underlying facts (messes) that have prevented them from attaining successful sustainable weight loss in the past.

The mess: A life of putting energy into everything but yourself in an attempt to gain acceptance and love.

The message: You have to learn to love yourself.

Action step: Every night this week, before you go to sleep, recite at least three things that you love about yourself.

Journal

Today's date is:

Here are ten things that I love about myself:

"You're a beautiful mess."
— Anonymous

The Rolling Stones

The Rolling Stones

Chapter 10

Sarah E.'s Story: Creating Community

Born in Chertsey, England

Fun fact: Sarah always carries a stash of motivational wrist cuffs that she has designed, so that she can give them to anyone she thinks may need a lift. She also makes a mean curry, collects antiques, and has an extensive knowledge of underground house music.

Sarah and I have many mutual friends, as we attend many of the same social functions and events. We've both been active on social media for several years, and our contact online makes it feel as if we've known each other for quite some time. Sarah has the type of personality that makes people feel instantly comfortable. She has a raw authenticity about her because she always shares from her heart. From a wealthy family in England, she carries none of the airs that you may presume she ought to have; she is down to earth and friendly to everyone she meets.

Sarah is a breath of fresh air. It is obvious through watching her interactions with friends on social media that she is deeply loved.

Date 10 — What is the mess that became your message?

Moving to Washington, D.C. from London with her first husband brought on "three years of mess." Sarah felt isolated, without her tribe of girlfriends, in a culture that was very different from London. Feeling alone, Sarah realized that it was up to her to create her own community. She did this by attending events around the city. She went to art openings, shows, and a variety of social and cultural events. She did what she could to get herself out there.

She came to see that while she was able to do this, not all women feeling isolated are able to do what she did, as many women do not feel comfortable making such in-person efforts.

The message that Sarah received from the mess is that she needed to create a community that is easy to access, for women who like to discuss a variety of issues in a supportive, non-judgmental environment — a group with a *team* type of feel. In 2019, Sarah created the Facebook Group *Ladies Who Listen* — a private group that, as of this writing, has 1.3K members and is still growing. The intention of the group is to widen the support net for women who don't have friends or family nearby or who would simply like to discuss various issues with women outside of their immediate circle.

Through the mess, Sarah's message is having a positive effect on the quality of life for many women on a daily basis. Her timing could not have been more perfect, as she created this group just months before the universal struggles of the pandemic began.

The mess: Feeling isolated and alone without a community of support.

The message: We create our own community — and there are a number of effective vehicles to do so.

Action step: Commit to attending an upcoming event, or invite a new friend out for coffee. Do something social that is outside of your comfort zone.

Journal

Todays date is:

Although its possibly scary, I will grow my community by at least three new friends this year, by doing the following:

"A messy kitchen is a sign of happiness."
— Anonymous

Chapter 11

Paige's Story: Finding Grace

Born in Tyler, Texas

Fun fact: A concert pianist and graduate of The Juilliard School of Music, Paige plays exclusively classical music; however, her choice of music to listen to is hard rock, hip-hop, and country. She loves the English rock band Radiohead.

Paige and I met approximately twelve years ago when our children attended the same grade school. While our children weren't in the same class, Paige and I saw each other almost daily, standing among the other parents outside of school, waiting for our young children. If my memory serves me correctly, we had a chance to socialize at an event that was a buy-in party offered up at the school's annual auction, and that is where our friendship really kicked off.

Date 11 — What is the mess that became your message?

At the beginning of our virtual date, Paige shared these words that had not yet been shared by any of the women I had spoken to during this project. She said, "Not all messes clean up in a mindful manner."

After graduating from The Juilliard School in New York City, Paige lived a life that fascinates me: the life of a working artist. While living in the Big Apple, through her 20s and early 30s, she performed across Europe and America. She was an incredibly successful concert pianist. During quarantine, Paige shared some of her music on Facebook, which brought me to tears. It provided me with a glimpse into her exceptional talent.

In her late 30s, Paige met her husband. He was perfect. He was kind, he had a successful career, and he also wanted a family. Paige decided to quit performing to become the perfect wife and mom, dedicating her life to her family. She had two lovely daughters, lived in a gorgeous house, moved from the East Coast to Seattle for her husband's job, and jumped right into life as the picture-perfect mom. From the outside, she was living a dream life.

For twelve years, Paige didn't play any music at all. Her seemingly perfect life began throwing her curve balls — cancer, a battle with alcoholism, and divorce. Going back to Paige's original words — that not all messes clean up in a mindful manner — Paige explained further that "some of our messes are messier than others. Sometimes our messes clean up quick, nice and neat; other times, the clean-up itself can be messy. And then there are some messes that can't really be cleaned up, but they can become messages over the passing of time."

Through the process of her healing, after twelve long years, Paige has taken up playing the piano again. Her love for the piano returned — this time, without the pressure she felt in her younger years. Paige's story reminds me that we need to be gentle with ourselves when messes happen.

The mess: Giving up a career for a seemingly picture-perfect life, which is eventually rocked by cancer, alcoholism, and divorce.

The message: Some of our messes are messier than others. Even the clean-ups can be messy; and sometimes the messages from the messes take a long time to sink in. Therefore, let's be gentle with ourselves during and after the mess. Let's give ourselves some grace.

Action step: Give yourself the gift of grace this week: Be gentle and patient with yourself.

Journal

Todays date is:

Here are the messes from which I still havent figured out all the messages . . . but I trust that they will become clear over time:

"The reality is, people mess up.
Don't let one mistake ruin a
beautiful thing."
— Anonymous

Chapter 12

Jane's Story: Rejecting Stereotypes

Born in Chicago, Illinois

Fun fact: In 1970, Jane was in the ninth grade and president of the student council of her junior high school. She returned from Winter Break wearing a pant suit and was promptly detained. Her mother was called and advised to bring her daughter a skirt. Jane's mother called the ACLU and was told that the school district had lost *Poll v. Seattle Public Schools* (a case in which Tom Poll had sported a Beatles haircut, and a local high school suspended him). The next day, the district received a directive from the school president saying that they could not compel girls to wear skirts and dresses exclusively. The dress code changed for girls and female teachers on the first day of the second semester, later that month. Jane didn't know that teachers had been included in that decision until years later, when she ran into one of her former teachers, who thanked her.

Jane and I met over fifteen years ago at a fitness class held at a mixed martial arts school located in North Seattle. I eventually began teaching the class and Jane was a regular attendee. She and I got to know each other not just through the class, but also through social media. Watching Jane on social media, I have enjoyed her dry wit and her observations of life along with her refreshing candor.

Date 12 — What is the mess that became your message?

When we spoke on our date, it happened to be during a time of quite a bit of civil unrest in Seattle. Anarchists under the guise of Black Lives Matter and law enforcement officers were clashing nightly. Our city mirrored the divide that was happening across the country.

Always prepared, a former journalist, Jane knew the question I was poised to ask and the mess she planned to share. The mess she told me about has in part made her who she is today. The mess we spoke of is: *stereotypes.* Jane remembers that at just seven years of age, when she and her family moved to North Seattle, as the only Black girl in her grade-school class, she decided that she was not going to allow stereotypes to define her.

Looking back on her life, Jane realizes that some of her choices were made in part because they did not fit the stereotype of what a Black child should do. She was raised by a mother who was an incredible pianist, a prodigy, in fact — but who was not able to become a professional classical pianist because it wasn't a profession in which Black people were welcome. Jane did not mention this, but as I think back to the venues that would have featured classical pianists in the era when her mom played, most of those venues would not have allowed Black patrons in, let alone a Black artist.

Jane studied violin as well as the Martha Graham style of modern dance — two arts that did not have many Black children studying. She recalls growing up in the Leschi neighborhood of Seattle — a neighborhood known for homes that have beautiful views of Lake Washington. Jane recalls White friends coming over and being surprised that the house she lived in was an attractive custom home with a lake view — not the type of home that they expected their Black friend to live in. In college, Jane joined a sorority, where she was the only Black pledge member. Now, she sits on that sorority's national Diversity Inclusion and Access Committee.

The message that Jane received from the mess that stereotypes brought was to trust in herself. She opened herself up to possibilities, not allowing herself to be defined by any stereotype. Jane has used stereotypes as a vehicle to propel her to be anything and everything she wants to be, rather than seeing them as roadblocks that hold her back. Many times during her life, she was the one Black person in the room — whether it was at a violin recital, a dance recital, a sorority event, or the workplace. By trusting in herself and living her life on her own terms, she has contributed to breaking stereotypes by example — something that her young-adult daughter has continued.

The mess: Stereotypes.

The message: Use stereotypes as your motivation to be yourself. Do not let society put you in a box.

Action step: Think about the messages that you've received throughout your life because of stereotypes, and remind yourself that you don't have to believe them or live by them.

Journal

Today's date is:

The messages of who I should be because I am a woman; because I am Black, White, Asian, or Latino; because I am short, tall, fat, or skinny; because I am a brunette, a blonde, or a redhead; and so on — whatever the stereotypes are — these do not define me. I am:

Chapter 13

Jiawen's Story: Defining My Own Expectations

Born in Shanghai, China
Fun fact: Jiawen's favorite movie is *Casablanca*.

Jiawen and I met just this past year through a mutual friend. I immediately found Jiawen's friendly nature and her easy conversational style a delight. Since that initial meeting, we've gotten together for virtual meetings during the COVID-19 pandemic; we took an outdoor walk together; became members of the same non-profit board, and we've shared several fun and friendly text messages. Jiawen is from Shanghai, China — a city my family and I visited during the summer of 2014. It happens to be one of my top five favorite cities that I've had the opportunity to visit. I'm sure much of my love for the city stems from my daughter being adopted from China; but it was also the beauty and the mixture of old China and new Western-influenced China that brought Shanghai to life for me.

Date 13 — What is the mess that became your message?

It was fascinating to speak with Jiawen about what life was like growing up in Shanghai. She attended an elite boarding school from the age of eleven to eighteen. Each class had approximately 120 students, which is small considering these children come from a city of 24.5 million citizens. It is acclaimed as the best school in all of Shanghai — one that only a select few are invited to test into, and of those invited only a few make the cut. It is one of those schools where parents know that if their child is admitted, a future paved with success is almost certainly guaranteed. The children are truly the best and the brightest in Shanghai, training to become diplomats. Without a doubt, there are very high expectations placed on these children.

The children are constantly told that they are special, and because they are special, it is imperative that they perform and live up to their expectations. Jiawen's entire self-worth as a child attending an elite school was based on her performance in school. Being raised this way, she began her adult life believing that she needed to perform perfectly in school and in her career to have value.

After graduating from that boarding school, Jiawen moved to the other side of the world — to McMinnville, Oregon, as an exchange student while attending Linfield College. At the time, not many Chinese college students were studying abroad in the US. As someone who was trained to be the best, with her self-worth based on external measures, a single major was not enough. Jiawen chose to double major in computer science and finance — two majors with course requirements that had nothing in common. Therefore her studies were rigorous, and she spent very little time on extra-curricular activities or socializing. After graduating from college, she pursued a career in finance and rose through the ranks. It wasn't until she was in her late 20s that life became a little messy.

While those messy years were arguably also her most fun years, she felt lost for the first time in her life. She was not doing what she was supposed to do. Instead, as she considered moving into an MBA program, she spent her time going out nightly with friends and networking. She gave up her job in finance. This period of self-discovery brought with it some guilt, which she experienced because she'd left the path she had been conditioned to take.

Through this mess, the message was that she needed to break from the expectations that were grounded in her childhood. She says that learning this message — not to rely on external factors for her self-worth — has made her a better mother. While she expects her daughter to do her best, she encourages her to explore, so that she can find what she loves, without it being dictated to her by others.

The mess: A childhood filled with expectations and judgment from external sources as a measure of self-worth.

The message: Break away from the expectations established during your childhood, which no longer serve you. You can define and forge your own path.

Action step: Recite this mantra: "I am free to be myself!"

Journal

Todays date is:

Here are the childhood messages that no longer serve me. I will replace them with these positive affirmations:

"Please excuse the mess.
The kids are making memories."
— Anonymous

Chapter 14

Melissa's Story: Filling My Own Cup

Born in South Bend, Indiana
Fun fact: Melissa can sing the alphabet backwards while standing on her head!

Melissa and I met when we were eighteen years old, the age that our youngest children are now. We met each other on the first day of our freshman year of college, both assigned to the same dorm floor at a Quaker college located in Newberg, Oregon. You wouldn't picture us as naturally drawn to one another, since Melissa was raised in Wichita, Kansas and I grew up in inner-city Seattle — but we hit it off immediately. Eventually, we became roommates in the second part of the school year. While we ended up attending school together for just that one year (Melissa transferred to a new college after the first year), we've remained life-long friends — even bridesmaids at each other's weddings.

Date 14 — What is the mess that became your message?

Some messes slowly creep up over time. This one crept up over a decade. Melissa was staying at home, taking care of two young children close in age. Then one day, she realized that she was living a life that felt void of passion. Somewhere along the way, she'd lost the spirit that she used to have before marriage. In Melissa's words: "I had nothing filling my own cup."

At the time of our virtual date, Melissa had been divorced for about a year, after being married for over twenty years. She told me about the evolution of finding herself during her marriage. She realized that after staying home with her children for several years, she needed to find her own identity and self-worth. For years, she had been going through the motions of a happy life with her family without personally feeling fulfilled.

At one point during her search to find something that was all her own, she was driving past a retirement home, and spontaneously pulled over to ask about volunteer opportunities. Soon she was volunteering at activity time, including helping with Wii Bowling. She especially enjoyed time with her favorite partner, a resident at the retirement home whom she teamed up with to win many of the virtual bowling tournaments. Volunteering at the retirement home, she realized, helped to fill her very empty cup. By getting involved in this way, she was reminded that she needed something outside of her home life to contribute to; so she eventually decided to find a paying job outside of the home. Fortunately, the job she found was in presentation and sales, which was a natural fit for her outgoing personality. She felt her cup begin to fill.

Now, although admittedly feeling nervous at times — being newly single and making it on her own — she is living more in the present moment than ever before. To Melissa's surprise, when she mentioned at a family dinner that she was going to be speaking with me and that the subject matter was *a mess that became a message,* her young-adult daughter shared that in the last twelve years, this is the first time she has ever seen her mom actually enjoying life. She said that she truly sees that her mom is no longer just going through the motions. Melissa had been just killing time for so many years; she was down, she had anxiety, and she had settled for a life without passion. Unbeknownst to her, all of what she had been feeling had been visible to her daughter. She was grateful that her daughter had noticed her transformation.

The mess: Going through the motions of life instead of fully embracing a full life.

The message: While we love our children and know that our job of being a mother is important, we also have to find something that fills our own cup if we want to live a life filled with purpose and passion.

Action step: This week, upon waking up in the morning, take a moment to notice if you feel excited for the day ahead of you or if your cup feels empty.

Journal

Todays date is:

These are activities outside of my role as a wife and a mother (or outside of my job or career) that are my very own:

"Don't mind the mess."

— Anonymous

Chapter 15

Caron's Story: Taking Time to Grieve

Born In Swindon, England
Fun fact: It will surprise many people to learn that although Caron appears to be an extrovert, she is actually 100 percent an introvert.

Caron and I met over social media. She carries my husband's surname. We connected online after a member of her family and my father-in-law connected through genealogy research, which led to the discovery that several generations prior, a Leid from Scotland had immigrated to Trinidad, the nation where Caron's parents are both from. Caron and I have found that we have many things in common, including December birthdates that are just a few days apart.

Date 15 — What is the mess that became your message?

The mess that Caron and I discussed stems from her late 20s, when she lost the man she loved to cancer. Caron was only twenty-seven years old when she experienced his untimely loss of her fiancé, which left her empty. The man she was going to marry was a professional football player. He was young and healthy — certainly not someone she expected to lose before they could begin their life together.

Caron, during her grief, met another man whom she would end up having a fifteen-year relationship with, ten of those years in marriage. She knew for much of the relationship that it was not the right fit. Looking back on her marriage, she realizes now that she should have given herself time to grieve before getting into a new relationship. While her marriage produced the love and pride of her life — her handsome and smart son — she sees now that she never should have made such a major decision, committing to a new relationship before she allowed herself the time she needed to grieve.

Caron provided me with the following analogy: "When the rug is pulled out from under you, you're like a battery that is at a zero charge. When someone comes along and provides you with a ten-percent charge, it feels great — but that is only because you were at empty. So even ten percent seems like it is something worth holding onto."

The message she got from the mess is to allow time to heal and grieve. Caron has carried this message through to cope with other losses in her life — most recently the loss of her beloved mom who suffered for years with Alzheimer's disease. Knowing that she is still in the grief stage of loss, Caron is choosing not to make major decisions during this time. She recognizes that she needs to wait until she completes her own "charge." She knows that strength can be found in the quiet of being alone while healing from a loss.

The mess: Heartache after losing someone you deeply love.

The message: Allow yourself the time you need to grieve the loss before making any major decisions.

Action step: Get out of your head this week and take time to notice how your heart feels.

Journal

Today's date is:

I will allow myself time to properly grieve about:

"Messy hair — don't care."

— Anonymous

Chapter 16

Jennifer's Story: Learning the Importance of Self-Care During a Pandemic

Born in Reston, Virginia
Fun fact: Jennifer is a self-described terrible dancer, but she doesn't let that stop her from getting her groove on!

Nearly fifteen years have passed since I first met Jennifer. We met on a girls' weekend trip to Vail, Colorado. Jennifer was invited by my girlfriend whom she was working with at the time, and we have since been on at least three other girls' trips together over the years. When you meet Jennifer, you immediately feel enveloped in kindness. Her caring presence makes her a very easy person to talk to. We have a bond of not just being moms but also of being mothers of both biological and adopted children. It has been good to share our experiences with one another over the years.

Date 16 — What is the mess that became your message?

The mess for Jennifer that recently came front and center was the anxiety she experienced during the COVID-19 pandemic and civil unrest of 2020. As a busy career woman and mother of three, Jennifer has historically put aside self-care as a priority. When the pandemic hit our country and many states issued stay-at-home orders — with businesses closing and unemployment skyrocketing — Jennifer, who describes herself as someone prone to anxiety, definitely felt that anxiety creep in.

Not wanting the anxiety to overtake her, Jennifer was forced to recognize the powerful effect that ignoring the anxiety could have on her daily life. So she decided to take affirmative steps to make self-care a priority.

As 2020 progressed, Jennifer learned to approach life in a more relaxed manner. Setting her intention to let life happen instead of trying to control it has allowed her to accept and adapt to change in a much gentler way. The practice of self-care that she has adopted due to the mess of 2020 — which has included carving out time to exercise at home, take hikes, and check in with family members — has added to her life in such a positive way that she plans to carry the habit forward after the pandemic is contained and we get back to "normal," whatever that may look like.

Jennifer's story reminds me that sometimes things have to get bad to show us where our priorities need to be. Now that Jennifer is taking the time she needs for self-care, it is providing her with the peace of mind and the necessary tools to handle the stress that comes her way.

The mess: Increased anxiety during the pandemic.

The message: Self-care is important when things get messy. It allows us to handle the mess without experiencing overwhelming anxiety.

Action step: Schedule an outdoor walk with a girlfriend.

Journal

Todays date is:

Self-care doesnt have to cost a thing. Here is a list of some things I enjoy — things Ill do this week to take care of myself:

"Excuse the mess."

— Anonymous

Chapter 17

Kathryn's Story: Realizing That We Can All Grow and Change

Born in Denver, Colorado
Fun fact: Kathryn's next chapter in life, one that she has recently begun, is working as a playwright.

Kathryn and I met through our children. My son and daughter attended the same small independent grade school as Kathryn's daughter. It feels like a lifetime ago given that all three children are now attending out-of-state colleges.

Date 17 — What is the mess that became your message?

For Kathryn, one of life's biggest messes stemmed from growing up with a very abusive dad and not being protected — or even initially believed — by her mom. Kathryn was devastated by the response of the person who was supposed to protect her. Her mother's failure led to years of a very damaged relationship between mother and daughter, including a period of estrangement.

Recognizing that she needed to heal from the abuse that she grew up with, Kathryn went to work on healing herself. During her process of healing, she realized that she did not need to "time travel" to the painful memories of childhood every time she thought of or saw her mom. With a lot of self-study and various therapies, including hypnosis, she was able to truly comprehend that she was no longer the same person that she was as a child or as a younger adult.

Through this healing, Kathryn learned that after her father died, her mother had also worked diligently on her own growth and healing; thus, her mom had become a stronger more self-aware person. At a family gathering, which took place a few years after her dad died, her mom pulled Kathryn aside to talk to her in a separate room. To Kathryn's surprise, her mom apologized and admitted where she had failed. In the past, her mom would have never taken time away from a family party to talk to Kathryn, let alone acknowledge where she'd failed as a mother.

Kathryn's story reminds me that while we can often recognize our own growth and change, we forget that those around us — especially those whom we've had conflicts with, even our very own parents — can also grow and change. We have to be able to grant them that understanding. For Kathryn, that recognition, and the grace that she was able to provide to her mom, gave her the best two years she'd ever had with her mother before she passed away. That's two years that Kathryn would never have been able to experience if she hadn't decided to give her mom the gift of acknowledging that she also had the ability to grow and change.

The mess: An abusive dad and a mom who didn't have the strength to protect her young daughter.

The message: Give others the kindness of understanding that they have the ability to grow and change.

Action step: Reach out to someone from your past whom you had a disagreement with; grant them the favor of recognizing that they have also grown and changed.

Journal

Todays date is:

I havent spoken to ____________________ because of a conflict we had years ago, but I am going to either reach out in person, or keep that individual in my thoughts today — focusing on grace, forgiveness, and understanding. Here's whats on my mind about that:

"I'm not a hot mess –
I'm a spicy disaster."
— Anonymous

Chapter 18

Gage's Story: Becoming a Role Model

Born in Tacoma, Washington
Fun fact: You don't want to cross Gage. She is an accomplished black belt in karate.

I remember Gage as a child. Her mom and I met when Gage was about five years old. When I look back through the years at the few times I had the opportunity to see Gage, I remember her being on the quieter side, very sweet, and polite. Now at twenty-six, Gage is a YouTube sensation and podcaster — a young woman who has touched many lives over the last few years with her authenticity, intelligence, and humor, sharing her journey as a transgender woman. Her videos are raw, frankly taking her audience through her journey as a young transgender woman in transition.

Date 18 — What is the mess that became your message?

At age ten, Gage knew she was different from other boys her age. She internalized the feelings of being different and did not have the confidence or even the language to express who she was. Social media wasn't available. YouTube was just beginning and was not the popular informational medium that it is now. Her teen years were a time of much internal conflict, which she experienced on her own.

Thankfully, much has changed since Gage was a teenager. There are now role models for trans teens, people who can be found online through social media and mainstream media. Discussions of what it means to be transgender can be seen, although still sparse, on mainstream media. For Gage, growing up without such external tools available to understand her identity contributed to her not being able to express herself until early adulthood.

It was during her second year of college that she found the words to identify and share what she had known for a long time: that she is a transgender woman. Initially, her biggest concern was hurting her parents. She thought about how hard it might be for them to learn that their child was transgender. However, to her great relief, her parents supported her from day one — including eventually sharing a piece of their journey on Gage's YouTube channel of their experience as parents of a transgender person.

Through the difficulty of growing up without the resources to understand what it meant to be transgender, the message that arose from the *mess* of figuring it out on her own has become a *gift* to so many young adults. Gage has chosen to publicly share her journey to help other transgender youths and young adults who are lacking support, and she answers their questions. Based on her YouTube and podcast following, the communications she receives, and some of the recognition that she experiences when she is out in public, it is clear that she has touched many lives. She continues to inspire and motivate young people, helping others to feel confident about who they are.

The mess: Growing up as a transgender child without the resources, language, or role models to identify with.

The message: We can take the difficult experience of growing up without the right resources, and tell others about our journey openly and honestly, so that they can find a place of support and conversation as they journey through their own self-discovery.

Action step: Think about what tough experiences you have had that could help another person in a similar situation who may be struggling to find their place in the world.

Journal

Todays date is:

I know I can be a role model for others because:

"I'm not even a hot mess
anymore…I'm just a mess.
Room temp."
— Anonymous

Chapter 19

Sarah R.'s Story: Challenging Myself

Born in Pomona, California
Fun fact: Michael Franti's *Say Hey* is her favorite song.

Sarah and I met during our first year of law school, which means that we've known each other for over half of our lives. We also worked together right out of law school as deputy prosecutors. Since then, marriages and children have happened — we lived through our 30s and 40s, and now we're navigating our 50s. All this time, I never realized Sarah suffered from an anxiety disorder until she shared this with me on our Zoom date.

Date 19 — What is the mess that became your message?

Successful, beautiful, smart, and kind — what could possibly be the mess? The mess was a lifetime of anxiety. Anxiety was something that wasn't spoken of much while Sarah was growing up — and it wasn't until a diagnosis in her 30s that she realized that she had been living with an anxiety disorder for her entire life. The disorder stunted her self-confidence and kept her in a place where she was spending so much time focusing on possible worst-case scenarios, trying to figure out answers, and attempting to control outcomes, that it was interfering with her ability to fully enjoy life. As she explained, "Sometimes when you suffer from anxiety, because you are always trying to control the outcomes, you focus on all the negativity — the 'what can go wrong' — which takes away your ability to enjoy the positives that are all around you."

After experiencing a few episodes of what she now knows were anxiety attacks, and developing a temporary muscle twitch, Sarah began a frightening diagnostic journey that finally culminated in the correct diagnosis of anxiety disorder. Understanding her diagnosis, she decided that she needed to learn how to manage the anxiety so that she could live her life to the fullest.

Part of managing her anxiety includes constantly challenging herself to experience new things — like jumping into ice-cold water to participate in a Polar Bear Plunge event; taking up running in her 40s; learning to macramé; taking Spanish lessons; volunteering for pro bono clinics in areas of law outside her regular practice; trying challenging recipes; and teaching community college classes. She continues to set ongoing challenges for herself so that she doesn't become paralyzed by anxiety. Each time she experiences something new, no matter how big or small, she is reminded that no matter what life throws her way, she will be okay.

Once she started to work on managing her anxiety, Sarah began to see how privileged her life had been. She grew up in a good home, and money was not an issue; she attended good schools, she earned a law degree, and she has been generally healthy all of her life. Taking the time to realize how blessed her life has been helps her release the anxiety, reminding her not to focus on the negatives of every situation — the "what could go wrong" moments of thought.

Nowadays, Sarah talks openly about her anxiety and shares her experience with others if she ever learns that they are struggling with anxiety, too. She encourages people with anxiety to talk about it with a counselor if they need to, and to take anti-anxiety medication, if necessary. Medication is something Sarah does not need to take most of the time but she recognizes that there are moments when life gets messy, and she accepts the fact that sometimes she can benefit from the extra support.

The mess: Living with anxiety disorder.

The message: You can't control everything. When you challenge yourself by doing something outside of your comfort zone, your experiences will teach you that no matter what, you will be okay.

Action step: Sign up for a new class, a 5K run/walk, or something else you haven't tried before. Or, simply challenge yourself to speak to someone new today.

Journal

Todays date is:

Today I challenge myself to: ___

This is out of my comfort zone but I know I can do it. I will complete this challenge by taking the following steps:

"I'll see your hot mess and raise you a walking disaster."
— Anonymous

Chapter 20

Susan's Story: Finding the Silver Lining

Born in Salem, Oregon
Fun fact: Susan lived in Ecuador for a semester during college and speaks fluent Spanish — although she's a little out of practice these days.

Susan and I met eight years ago at one of author Martha Brockenbrough's book signings. Martha is one of our many mutual friends. I remember the time period in which we met, because I was recovering from my first of two hip-replacement surgeries and I had recently closed my fitness training studio. I recall recommending Susan's studio to some of my former clients after hearing fabulous reviews about her fitness classes, which many of my girlfriends were regularly attending. My girlfriends who knew Susan raved about her workout classes and sang her praises — not only because of the amazing workouts she had developed but because they loved her humor and energy.

Date 20 — What is the mess that became your message?

Susan is an easy person to talk to. She began our virtual date by commenting that there are messes that we create, and messes that simply happen to us through no fault of our own. And with this as a premise, she went on to say, "The message is that through all messes, a message can be found."

While she's not a believer that everything happens for a reason, Susan does believe that with everything that happens, there are always options. She points out that you can look for a silver lining — or at the very least find a way to make the best out of the mess.

One of Susan's favorite sayings, something she shares with her daughters is, "You just never know what is around the corner." What appears one day to be a mess can be an opening for something greater. As Susan's grandmother used to say to her, "Susie, you've got to get behind yourself and push!"

I recently witnessed Susan's resilience and can-do attitude when our state went into lockdown because of the COVID-19 pandemic. Part of the lockdown regulations included shutting all gyms. On the day of the shutdown she immediately went into action, creating a Facebook group, which quickly grew to 1.1K members before she moved it to a separate online platform. Susan led live online workouts and posted these daily on the Facebook group page. She was the voice that motivated and helped her many followers through the difficulties of navigating the COVID-19 shutdown.

Susan wasn't only worried about her business but she also carried a lot of concern for her clients, whom she knew depended on their daily workouts with her — not just for their physical wellbeing but also for their mental wellbeing. It is not a surprise to me that she was concerned for her clients' mental wellbeing during the stressful times of the COVID-19 shutdown. When she established her studio years ago, she chose to call it "Strength Studio" for the mental strength that results from challenging yourself physically.

Susan found the silver lining in the mess. She plans to continue her online platform even after her gym is able to fully re-open. She found that while the online platform was a response to a mess, it created a place that now is relied upon by hundreds of her clients. And that is just one example of how Susan moves forward despite the messes life throws her. Not only that, her resilience also inspires others who receive their messages simply by watching Susan and observing the positive way she handles life's inevitable messes.

The mess: Life is always messy.

The message: A silver lining can be found in every mess, even if some linings are thinner than others.

Action step: When things go sideways this week — even the little things — actively look for the silver lining in the mess.

Journal

Todays date is:

Although this turned out to be messy today, I found the silver lining in:

"My room isn't messy;
it's an obstacle course
designed to keep me fit."
— Anonymous

Chapter 21

Linda's Story: Letting Go of the To-Do List

Born in Chicago, Illinois

Fun fact: Linda, who was ranked in the top twenty in the State of California for Women's Cross Country in high school, was recruited to Chapman University. When she arrived at school, the program had been cancelled. Due to the cancelled program, she tried out for the Women's Soccer team — despite having never been trained in the sport — and she made the team. She ended up playing all four years for the school.

Linda and I met about three years ago when we were both working on a local non-profit campaign. Linda has such an outgoing and friendly nature that I found it easy to talk to her from the moment we met. She is a consummate connector. I know so many women who have met one another through Linda. She loves bringing people together. She is active in the community — a living example of how one person can make a difference.

Date 21 — What is the mess that became your message?

While the way that Linda lives life has made her the successful career woman she is, it also became her mess.

Linda is someone who has always dreamed big. She has never limited herself — slaying goal after goal. Her résumé is something to behold, containing many diverse areas of success in leadership; it highlights her natural entrepreneurial skill, along with community activism. She is not someone who sits by the sidelines to watch life go by.

Linda's message from the mess came through a life scare in 2019: a stroke and a brain aneurysm that ruptured during surgery, leaving her to face months of difficult rehabilitation. She had been a young, seemingly healthy woman in her mid-40s. The message was clear: She needed to take better care of herself and put herself first. So, for the first time that she can remember — Linda started to limit her work hours, set boundaries, and take time for herself.

This powerful message has allowed Linda to become gentler with herself. She recites often, "It will get done tomorrow" whenever she is tempted to neglect taking much-needed downtime. Through the mess, a life with balance has emerged.

The mess: A life so busy that you forget to carve out time to care for yourself.

The message: Take time for yourself — and remember to tell yourself, whenever you are tempted to burn the candle at both ends, "It will get done tomorrow."

Action step: When you look at your to-do list this morning, take at least one thing off the list and save it for another day.

Journal

Todays date is:

I give myself permission to let go of my to-do list at least one day this week. And if that is too difficult, Ill start instead with a half day of free time this week — time carved out just for me, to do the following:

"Messy bun and getting stuff done."
— Anonymous

Chapter 22

Rose's Story: Taking on Life's Obstacles as They Come

Born in Seattle, Washington
Fun fact: Rose likes to juggle oranges!

I met Rose about fifteen years ago, at a fitness/lifestyle coaching certification course in Seattle, Washington. At the time, Rose's professional racing career was just taking off — *pun intended.* Thanks to social media, I have been able to watch her career expand over the years — from local to national sponsorships, and from being a local celebrity to becoming famous internationally.

Date 22 — What is the mess that became your message?

Rose's story of her mess really began for her as a child. As she explained, when you are the eighth child in a family of nine children, unless you are the Von Trapp family from the famed *Sound of Music,* home life will automatically be chaotic. It wasn't simply the sheer number of people in the house that caused the chaos. There were additional layers of dysfunction that manifested daily. With eleven mouths to feed, financial strain was constantly present. The house, located in Seattle, was already cramped for space, and her parents accumulated items. The home was filled to the brim, with nearly every surface taken — stacks of extra paper-route newspapers, plastic religious statues (duct-taped down in case of an earthquake), dirty dishes, board games with missing pieces, art supplies, or a random couch in the dining room covered in laundry.

Rose grew up literally navigating around obstacles. She also observed some of her older siblings struggle with depression and mental health challenges as they each carved out their own life journey, trying to make sense of the world around them.

Rose escaped the household chaos through athletics, playing soccer and other sports as a child. She found her passion in track racing. She is fast. Initially an indoor and outdoor collegiate track athlete at Georgetown University, she moved on to semi-professional racing after college. Rose experienced a pivotal moment in her racing career in 2016, when she competed to make the Olympic trials in the 800m, missing that year's qualifying mark by a mere five seconds.

While she was planning to train hard and try again in four years, a friend invited her to try a new challenge: obstacle-course racing. She figured, *Why not?* and ended up getting hooked! After a decade of racing around a track, attempting to hit perfect pacing splits, she found that running amok in the woods — jumping over, under, and through obstacles — sparked her spirit. She was in her element.

Rose has made her mess her message. She took a life skill learned at home during childhood — maneuvering through obstacles — to the professional level. Now, as a professional obstacle-course racer, she is a two-time American Ninja Warrior finalist, sponsored by a number of national companies. Conquering obstacles is no joke for Rose. Just as she did as a child, she trusts herself to be able to take on and overcome whatever comes her way. And, when times are good — when everything is going right — she doesn't worry about the next obstacle. She stays in the moment and enjoys the good times.

The mess: Growing up in a home filled with chaos, with both literal and figurative obstacles presenting constantly.

The message: Life is full of obstacles. Open yourself to enjoy the good moments, and don't be afraid of the next challenge. When things get bad, trust your instincts and believe that there is no obstacle you cannot hurdle.

Action step: Practice taking on obstacles as they come. There's always a way.

Journal

Todays date is:

Sometimes I feel like an obstacle racer. Whenever I encounter an obstacle, I will:

"Messy. Blessed. Life."

— Anonymous

Chapter 23

Maja's Story: Finding the Beauty — Even in the Darkness

Born in Bratislava, Slovak Republic
Fun fact: By the time she was just thirteen years of age, Maja was a five-time table tennis champion in the Slovak Republic's Table Tennis Women's Division.

I met Maja at a charity dinner several years ago. My husband and I were seated at the same table with her and her husband. I don't know if I mentioned that first meeting to her or if she even remembers it. Maja is one of those women who is purely memorable — striking and kind, she makes an unforgettable first impression. Several years after that charity event, one of our mutual girlfriends gifted me a shirt from Maja's clothing line, which set the ball in motion for our connection. I have since purchased one of her originally designed beautiful necklaces for a girlfriend who tragically lost her son. Choosing that handmade piece allowed me to experience first-hand the beauty and power of Maja's custom-made monogram jewelry designs.

Date 23 — What is the mess that became your message?

"Everything that I was afraid of ever happening to me, happened to me...."

As a teenager, Maja left her family in Slovakia and traveled the world as a model. When she arrived in the United States at just eighteen years of age, Maja had to face her fear of being alone. This turned out to be just one of many life fears that came her way. As Maja shared with me, just about everything she feared that could possibly happen, did.

She experienced a difficult pregnancy, which required her to face her fear of needles — because she had to self-administer treatments at home using needles. She also had to deal with the two most painful and unimaginable experiences a parent could ever have to face: the death of her daughter, Isabella, which was followed just a couple of years later with her three-year-old son being diagnosed with cancer.

Through all of these devastating experiences and losses, Maja realized that she was stronger than she ever imagined. She made it through these painful periods in life that she never thought she could survive. Through all of the heartache came her message of survival and strength.

As a child, Maja's passion and dream was to become an artist. She remembers that she had this dream and a love of art even at the tender age of five. She always loved art and fashion. Unfortunately, even as a child, she knew that these two areas weren't lucrative — let alone available career paths — in Slovakia. She therefore set her dream aside and focused on other less creative subjects in school.

It was after Isabella's death, when Maja began searching for a memorial piece of jewelry that she could wear to honor her daughter, that her childhood dream to be an artist in the fashion industry came to the surface. Unable to find a piece that felt suitable for her, she decided to design her own memorial pendant. Before long, she was designing beautiful jewelry for other people (www.majaarnold.com). Designing meaningful works of art for others, she found healing.

Since she began, Maja has designed over 700 necklaces, many of which are custom memorial pieces for people who have lost their children. And these pieces have brought so much healing to the recipients. Each one, hand-designed with care, is incredibly special and unique, made to represent a special personal bond that the custom pendant represents.

Maja reminds me that some messes, even the most painful ones, can bring a message that not only will change your own life — but can also be far-reaching to change the lives of everyone you touch.

The mess: Facing life's worst fears as they come to pass.

The message: Look for beauty even in the darkest of life's places, to design something beautiful.

Action step: At bedtime, each day this week, spend five minutes taking an inventory of the beauty you witnessed during the day.

Journal

Todays date is:

From some of my most painful life moments, I have found beauty in:

"Mess with me, I dare you."

— Anonymous

Chapter 24

Tee-Ta's Story: Breaking Free from Judgment

Born in Seattle, Washington

Fun fact: Tee-Ta is obsessed with eyebrows. She will not go anywhere without brushing her eyebrows. One time, after realizing that she had forgotten to brush her eyebrows before leaving the house, she made her friend stop at a store to pick up an eyebrow brush on the way to their intended destination.

Tee-Ta and I were introduced to each other about ten years ago through a mutual friend. When you meet Tee-Ta, it is very easy to forget that you just met because she so comfortably gels with everyone she meets. A lot has happened for both Tee-Ta and me in the past ten years. We each started our own businesses, she moved across the country from Washington state to Florida, and I've recently become an empty-nester.

Date 24 — What is the mess that became your message?

Knowing that I was going to ask her about a mess that became a message, Tee-Ta long considered the question prior to our virtual date. She shared with me that it is hard, if not impossible, to pick just one mess. As she pointed out, our lives are filled with messes — but the underlying message through all of life's messes is, "I am bigger than I think."

During the past year of the pandemic, Tee-Ta intentionally decided to let go of wasting time worrying about judgment from others. She has noticed that by letting go of worry, she is better able to move forward. She realizes that she is bigger than she thought — more able to affect the world around her than she ever thought possible. In addition to being a female business owner specializing in business branding, Tee-Ta has become even more visible by co-hosting a podcast called *Conversations with Tee-Ta and Tiffany: A Black Girl & A White Girl*, which is dedicated to facilitating courageous conversations about racism, inequities, and bias behaviors.

One of her favorite mantras is, "Great people do little things with excellence." According to Tee-Ta, she has learned that it is the little things that matter — the little things that are done when the spotlight isn't on and there isn't a crowd to watch. "It is the little things that show character." Her comment reminds me of a question that I have pinned on my office bulletin board, "If you could travel through the world with anonymity, what would you do?"

From conquering life's many messes, Tee-Ta has learned that she has resilience. She is now comfortable sharing herself with the world without the fear of judgment holding her back. She is ready to become big and live a life with purpose.

The mess: Living a small life where your fear of judgment by others is keeping you from living out your full purpose.

The message: Let go of the fear of judgment from others and start affecting the world around you with your many gifts.

Action step: Pull out a piece of paper this week, and each time you notice judgment creeping in — whether it be the fear of judgment from others or you judging yourself or others — make a note of it. Recognize how worrying about what others are thinking or doing is preventing you from living your best life.

Journal

Today's date is:

I can be my own worst enemy when it comes to living my purpose. I will stop the following behaviors or thoughts that are no longer serving me, and I will replace them with this list of positive, healthy thoughts and behaviors:

"Embrace messy hair."

— Anonymous

Chapter 25

Shay's Story: Resetting My Life During the Mess

Born in San Diego, California
Fun fact: A year after Shay was diagnosed with stage IV melanoma, she wrote to *The Oprah Winfrey Show*, thanking Dr. Oz for his segment on melanoma, which she credits for saving her life. A year after sending that message, she was asked to be a guest on Oprah's show to surprise Dr. Oz. It was Dr. Oz's last *Oprah* show appearance, before his own television show launched. It was a pivotal moment in Shay's life and one that she will never forget.

Shay and I met through our mutual girlfriends. Shay has a fabulous array of women in her life — women who have been together for years through thick and thin — and I've been fortunate to connect with and feel embraced by this amazing group of women. Over the years, I've learned that Shay is a true boss babe, with a heart of gold.

Date 25 — What is the mess that became your message?

Married for just one year, at age thirty-one, Shay received a devastating diagnosis: stage IV melanoma — an unimaginable mess.

On our virtual date, Shay described nine months of a very difficult treatment regimen, which involved a series of surgeries. Also, for a significant period of that nine months, the treatment included daily interferon doses. She shared a small laugh as she remembered that when she heard about the treatment plan, attempting to find something good in the mess, she pointed out that the one silver lining at the time was, "At least I'll lose weight on chemo." Unfortunately, the exact opposite happened: She gained eighty pounds in seven months. The interferon treatments, surgeries, and medicines proved very difficult for her body to manage.

Despite this physically challenging and mentally difficult time, Shay found a beautiful message in that mess. Relationships, including those with family members, were restored and grew stronger throughout the course of her grueling treatment. While cancer took a lot away from Shay, it also gave a lot back. She says it allowed her to "reset." She recognized that she had just one life to live, and she wasn't going to waste it.

Shay has continued to take messes and turn them into messages. Most recently, this past year of looking at the mess of the COVID-19 pandemic, she has used this time of social distancing as a new opportunity to reset. She has made time to work on her mental and physical health, finding balance between work, family, and self-care.

I love the idea that when life sends us messes, we can look at them as opportunities to reset rather than seeing them as barriers standing in our way.

The mess: A diagnosis of stage IV melanoma at only thirty-one years of age.

The message: Even the worst messes can be opportunities to reset.

Action step: Pinpoint an area in your life that could use a reset. Maybe it's your work life, family life, or spiritual life — or even a romantic relationship that could use some retooling. Do you need to ramp up your efforts regarding your health, nutrition, or physical fitness?

Journal

Todays date is:

The mess that happened in my life that gave me the opportunity to reset is:

"Take chances.
Make Mistakes.
Get Messy."
— Anonymous

Chapter 26

Mari's Story: Trusting My Intuition

Born in San Francisco, California
Fun fact: Mari met her husband on a dating app, over ten years ago!

Mari and I met through a year-long life coaching training program. Through online and in-person training, we got to know each other fairly well over a short period of time. Because of the nature of the training, we had conversations that were much more personal than what you would typically have in a new friendship.

Date 26 — What is the mess that became your message?

When I met Mari, she was a relatively recent Seattle transplant. She and her husband relocated from the Bay Area to the Seattle area for what she believed was her dream job, which included a nice bump up in pay. As it turned out, what she had hoped was her dream job turned out to be the mess. Then the job mess crossed over into her personal life, making her whole life feel like a mess.

The job she and her husband moved their entire life for felt like an exciting opportunity, because it felt as if the company had created the job just for her. But unfortunately she was sold a bill of goods that was never delivered. When she began her new position, she quickly realized that the department she was under lacked effective leadership. While the bad leadership was a challenge, the most difficult part of her daily interactions was the constant microaggressions she experienced. She was miserable. To add to the mess, her husband was laid off from his job. She felt stuck, because not only had she been responsible for uprooting them, now she was the sole breadwinner.

Fortunately, at long last Mari was able to leave that place, and today she is employed at a different company in a position she loves. She also enjoys building her life coaching business, knowing that her life experiences — even the unpleasant ones — have helped shape her into someone qualified to successfully understand and guide her clients. She was able to make the mess her message.

Here are three things she learned from that experience:

1. *Listen to your intuition.* There were several times, especially early into the job, where Mari suspected that the job really wasn't what she had been told it was, and she turned out to be correct.
2. *When feeling burdened, you can't keep the load.* You need to take care of yourself and get your control back, which includes asking for help, if needed. Don't hesitate to find someone to talk to — a trusted friend, a counselor, a mentor, or a life coach.

3. *It is okay to take baby steps.* You don't have to make a grand all-or-nothing move to improve your situation. Mari couldn't quit her job right away, but she found that she was able to take small steps towards eventually moving to a different environment with a position that fueled her soul.

While she certainly wouldn't want to relive the mess, Mari would be the first to tell you that she needed the mess to happen to get to where she is today.

The mess: Uprooting your life for your dream job, which turns into your nightmare job.

The message: Listen to your intuition, ask for help, and realize that taking small steps toward a better future even when you feel stuck is sometimes all you really need to push through.

Action step: Take a walk outside or simply sit outside and listen to your heart.

Journal

Todays date is:

Listening to my intuition, I know that there are baby steps I can take right now to move out of a less-than-ideal situation. The first two small steps I will take are:

"The messy bun is the crown
of the mom."
— Anonymous

Chapter 27

Alex's Story: Making Lemonade Out of Lemons

Born in Camarillo, California
Fun fact: Alex grew up on a small sheep farm, and she won the Sheep to Shawl contest at the local fair when she was thirteen years old.

Alex and I met about five years ago at one of our mutual girlfriend's parties. I've loved getting to know Alex. I adore her humor, her love of animals, her mad cooking skills, her appreciation of good wine, and her dedication to her friends and family. We share a number of mutual friends and the common words that I hear whenever her name is mentioned is, "I just love Alex."

Date 27 — What is the mess that became your message?

Alex's mess is every parent's worst fear. As life's messes often do, this one seemed to sprout up without warning. Her eldest son was two and a half years old and her younger son was a newborn.

She took both boys in for a routine well-baby appointment. Her family's regular pediatrician was not in the office and another pediatrician in the practice group was substituting that day. When the pediatrician reached out to touch the baby, Alex's older son — who had been told at home not to touch the baby because at such a young age he wasn't quite yet old enough to be gentle with a newborn — screamed out, "Do not touch the baby!" Trying to calm him and make him comfortable, the pediatrician spent a bit of time with him, showing her older son the stethoscope and explaining how it worked. It was during this chance interaction with her older son that the doctor heard something unusual — a heart murmur — which led to a referral to a cardiac specialist and the subsequent discovery of a serious heart defect.

And, just like that, the family's life was turned upside down. They became part of a group of parents of ill children, something they never could have predicted. Their young son required two heart surgeries to repair the defect. During her son's time at Seattle Children's Hospital, Alex witnessed all of the wonderful expressions of love that her son received from friends and family — including many gifts, especially Beanie Babies, which were all the rage at the time.

Alex noticed that some of the other children in the ICU were not only noticeably lacking gifts to fill their rooms, but also had no family with them. Alex remembers so clearly one little baby boy who was staying on the same floor as her son. He was from out of state. His mom was unable to travel, and his father was unable to make the trip until later in the baby's recovery. The baby not only was alone without family, he also did not receive the gifts that her son had received. After seeing these children whose families were in heartbreaking financial distress, Alex learned about the uncompensated care fund at Seattle Children's Hospital.

Alex turned her family's mess into not just a message but a mission. She brought her friends together and formed a guild to raise funds for uncompensated care. The guild she founded later became part of a larger guild also raising money for uncompensated care at Seattle Children's Hospital, The Preston Kuppe Guild (http://www.pkguild.org/Home/AboutUs). In addition to making it her mission to ensure that every child is able to receive care, Alex served on the Board of Trustees of Seattle Children's Hospital for nine years, and she still volunteers as a tour guide at the hospital and research facility.

I think about all the money that Alex has helped raised for children and families — people she will never meet. Alex reminds me that when a mess happens — even the worst imaginable painful mess — it can be turned into a message that can touch many lives.

Alex's son has now graduated from college and he is thriving, ready to take on the world.

The mess: Discovering your young child has a serious health condition.

The message: Something good can come out of even the worst of life's crises, so that you can help prevent the suffering of others.

Action step: Make lemonade out of lemons this week.

Journal

Todays date is:

Because of my own mess, I am in a unique position to recognize the needs of others. I can help by doing the following:

"People want to see the messy bits of your life."

— Anonymous

Chapter 28

Teri's Story: Enhancing Wellness and Longevity through Functional Nutrition

Born in Bellevue, Washington
Fun fact: Teri worked in Alaska in the fishing industry for two summers in college.

Teri and I met through a mutual friend at our friend's annual Favorite Things Holiday Party. Teri is strikingly beautiful. It isn't surprising that she is a nutrition and health coach because she is undeniably athletically fit, and her skin absolutely glows. She definitely practices what she preaches. She has been my go-to friend for any nutrition or supplement advice. Most recently, I reached out to her to seek food recommendations for a friend who was recovering after nearly a month on a ventilator due to COVID-19, and her wisdom was very helpful.

Date 28 — What is the mess that became your message?

On our virtual date, Teri told me about her dad. Teri's dad was her constant cheerleader. He meant the world to her. Her description of her dad made me think of my own father who passed away twenty years ago. I felt Teri's love and admiration for her dad come through very vividly as she described the man who had always been her rock.

During Teri's last year of college, her world came crashing down. While mowing the lawn, at just forty-eight years of age, her dad suffered a massive heart attack. The family would soon learn that his heart disease was so far advanced that he was not a transplant candidate. The dire news was absolutely devastating for the family. He would live just six more months following the heart attack. During those six months, he celebrated his forty-ninth birthday and was able to attend Teri's college graduation before passing away in his sleep.

After graduation, Teri became a pharmaceutical sales representative. She learned all that she could about cardiovascular disease and the pharmaceutical drugs available to treat it. She was very passionate about her job, hoping that she could provide the education and pharmaceuticals to help others who suffered from this horrible illness.

A life-long learner and ever curious, Teri's studies concerning the prevention of disease led her to look at holistic medicines, adding a great deal to what she had gleaned from Western medicine. When she first began this journey, it was believed that heredity was the leading contributing factor to heart disease, along with environment and lifestyle. Now, studies have shown that heredity may make up *only five percent* of determining the chances of dying from heart disease — with lifestyle choices and environment making up the rest.

After learning this, Teri began a two-decade quest for knowledge in the holistic medicine field, working with holistic practitioners. She eventually became certified herself as an Integrative Nutrition Practitioner. She now works one on one with her clients, providing them with the knowledge and tools to make healthy choices so that they can take control of their lives.

From the painful mess of losing her father, Teri made it her message and her passion to promote healthy living — so that hopefully another daughter will not have to experience the painful loss of her father from a disease that can be slowed or reversed by lifestyle changes. Because Teri continues to share with her clients and friends what she has so diligently studied, those touched by her message are able to choose to make wise lifestyle choices that are actually life-saving.

The mess: A beloved father dying too young from heart disease, which could have been prevented with different lifestyle and dietary choices.

The message: She learned all she could to help others — friends, family, and clients — to make smart lifestyle choices to prevent premature death.

Action step: For optimum health, up your water intake. This week, get yourself a good water bottle, and fill it up throughout the day. Notice how much better you feel.

Journal

Todays date is:

I have decided that I will take better care of myself. I am making this one lifestyle change today that will have a lasting impact on my longevity:

"Good moms have sticky floors, messy kitchens, laundry piles, dirty ovens, and happy kids."
— Anonymous

Chapter 29

Cati's Story: Letting Go of the Mess

Born in Bellingham, Washington
Fun fact: Cati is a personal trainer with a passion for fitness. As long as Cati is active, she is happy!

I was introduced to Cati a few years ago through her best friend from high school, Nancy. This past year, I got to know Cati even better when my husband and I were invited along with her and her husband for a week-long couples' trip to Cabo San Lucas, Mexico. Cati has always struck me as easygoing. After speaking with her on our Zoom date, I learned that what I perceive as her carefree attitude really stems from a specific intention that she sets daily to constantly move forward and to look for the positives in every situation.

Date 29 — What is the mess that became your message?

When we began our Zoom date, similar to many of the other women I spoke to, Cati immediately acknowledged that our lives are messy — we experience mess after mess. She pointed out that the message always exists in how we handle our messes.

Cati received her message on how to handle her messes by watching her dad. Her dad has always been a positive role model. She admires the way he manages life, with his focus on moving forward. He consistently chooses to focus on the positive, and not the negative. His positive attitude is obvious, considering he has battled with cancer — not just once, but five times. His exceptional mental strength has been a big part of what has gotten him through his difficult bouts with cancer, and his extraordinary strength has kept the family strong. Her father models what he has instilled in Cati: Don't revisit the messes. Always look forward, and look for the positive even in the most challenging moments.

She has raised her children in the same way. Cati's children have been raised to not be confined by restrictions and negativity but to always look forward to a bright future. Both of her children had challenging accidents and injuries that were beyond the normal scrapes and bumps of childhood, but Cati never dwelled on the injuries or possible limitations that could have come from these events. Instead, she and her husband have encouraged their children to keep an optimistic attitude, always moving forward. Now, both children are flourishing young adults — forging through the world, successfully conquering all of their own life messes.

I received so many messages from talking with Cati on our Zoom date. These can be applied to all of life's messes:

1. Do not become your mess. Don't let it define you.

2. Don't revisit your mess, or live in it. Keep your focus on the now and put your energy into moving forward towards a better future.
3. A positive mindset can be the game changer, even when you're faced with something as devastating as cancer.
4. Our kids learn how to deal with their life messes by watching how we deal with our own.

The mess: Life challenges, including health challenges, which could set anyone back.

The message: Don't become your mess; it does not define you.

Action step: Thank your mess for the lessons it has taught you. Then tell your mess that while it is a part of you and it has shaped you, it does not control you. Keep your eyes on a brighter future.

Journal

Today's date is:

I've let my mess define me for long enough. While it is a part of my history, it is not me and I will no longer allow it to limit me. Whenever I think of ______________________ I will turn my thought around to ______________________ instead, and move forward with this positive mindset:

"When something goes wrong in your life just yell "Plot Twist" and move on!"

— Anonymous

Chapter 30

Lilla's Story: Removing a Title Can Allow Room for Grace

Born in Redding, California
Fun fact: Lilla loves old country music. Classic artists like Patsy Cline are her favorites.

Lilla is my second cousin. We are almost ten years apart in age and she grew up in a different state than I did, so our interactions have been limited to the few and far between at large family reunions. Thanks to social media, we've gotten to know one another better in recent years. I've enjoyed watching her grow on social media into the inspirational woman that she is today. I was thrilled to have a chance to learn more about her on our virtual date.

Date 30 — What is the mess that became your message?

Lilla explained to me that her mess stemmed from childhood. Her dad was absent and an addict — failing to show up as a father time and time again. Lilla uses the word "painful" when describing her relationship with her dad. The pain she suffered as a child, growing up with a father she could not rely on, led her to making unwise and self-destructive life choices several times throughout her teenage years and as a young adult.

But as Lilla said, "there is purpose in pain."

Now, in her early 40s, her relationship with her dad, while not perfect, sits in a good place. What was the shift for her? She took away the title of *Dad* in her mind, and instead looked at him as she would any other person. In doing so, it removed all of her own expectations of who he should be and allowed her to see him as he is. Instead of labeling him with the title of *Dad,* Lilla saw him as someone's son — as someone who had a difficult childhood himself. Removing all expectations has allowed her to have empathy, to give him grace, and to recognize his strengths — in particular, his resilience.

A few weeks after our conversation, I saw a birthday post that Lilla made on Facebook for her dad, celebrating his kind heart, his ability to survive, his ingenuity, and his humor. It made me smile, realizing how far she has come in her relationship with him.

The message is that often our disappointment in others comes from our expectations of who we think they ought to be. If we can let go of the unrealistic expectations that we've created in our own mind, it opens up space to proceed with empathy and grace.

The mess: A painful childhood relationship with a father who struggled with addiction and his own demons.

The message: Taking away someone's title or label in your mind can allow you to have a deeper understanding — to see the person without judgment, as an individual with a unique journey rather than as a person taking on a role that you've expected them to play.

Action step: Over the next week, notice whenever you become upset with someone. Watch to see whether the reason you are troubled is because you aren't able to control their actions. Remind yourself that the only journey you have control over is your own.

Journal

Todays date is:

When I remove someone's title or label — mom/dad/brother/sister/child/etc. — my own expectations of that person will fall away, so that I can see their strengths. I will remove the title from the following family member so that I can see them in a new light:

"The truth is messy."

— Anonymous

Chapter 31

Shalonda's Story: Treating Everyone Like Family — A Lesson from My Mother

Born in Renton, Washington
Fun fact: Shalonda's favorite song of all time is *Sky Full of Stars* by Coldplay.

I found Shalonda on Instagram about three years ago when I was searching for a make-up artist for an event I was attending. Shalonda is one of the most talented make-up artists in the Seattle area. And her artistry expands beyond Seattle. She has become a representative for a number of make-up and beauty companies, sharing their products and her flawless application of them on social media (Instagram: @seattle_mua). She has grown a successful business on her own, becoming a national leader in the industry — a thriving social media influencer.

Date 31 — What is the mess that became your message?

I recall that during our first meeting, Shalonda and I spoke about her family. It was clear that she was raised in a very loving and close family. So I wasn't surprised when on our virtual date she chose to share that her mess was the painful loss of her mom.

Shalonda was blessed with a mother who embraced everyone. Her mom was warm and inviting. It never mattered to her mom what the color of someone's skin was, or if they were rich or poor, or what they were wearing — she simply and easily let people into her life and made them feel welcome. At Shalonda's mom's funeral service, when the minister asked her children to stand up, at least thirty people stood. That's how much love she poured out for the people who were so fortunate to have met her. It gives me goosebumps to picture that moment at the funeral service.

While Shalonda's mom's death was a shock to the community, it was an absolutely devastating time for Shalonda. A sudden brain aneurysm, which caused her mom's death, was something no one could prepare for. The mess of her mom's death propelled Shalonda to take on much of her mom's message: to encourage women.

Shalonda has taken this message to heart through her work as a gifted make-up artist and influencer. She not only helps women see their external beauty, but as she carves out time to really be present with each of her clients, she makes an effort to connect at a heart level. She shares the welcoming spirit that was planted by her mom.

Just like her mother, Shalonda is warm and inviting, never caring about the color of someone's skin or whether the person is wealthy or poor. Instead, she sees the beauty in everyone she meets. With her unique skill and originality, Shalonda brings out not only the outer beauty but also the inner glow of all of her clients.

The mess: Suddenly losing a beloved parent.

The message: My parent's greatest gifts can live on through me.

Action step: Think about one message that you have learned from your mom or dad, or from a guardian or mentor — and take an affirmative step this week to share that message in your words or actions.

Journal

Todays date is:

While______________________ whom I dearly loved, is no longer with me on this Earth, their spirit can live on through me. I can carry on their legacy by:

"Beginnings are always messy."
— Anonymous

Chapter 32

Carrie's Story: Opening Myself Up to Opportunity

Born in Edmonds, Washington
Fun fact: Carrie has been a vegan for the past seventeen years, since she was thirty-three. She chose to be a vegetarian at the tender age of thirteen.

Carrie and I met when we were in our early 20s. I was an intern attorney in my last year of law school and Carrie was a Victims' Advocate — both of us working for the Pierce County Prosecutor's Office in Tacoma, Washington. It is hard to believe that we've known each other for half of our lives. In recent years, Carrie and I reconnected after she moved back to Washington state subsequent to living for several years out of state and even out of country. She had been moving from place to place for quite awhile with her former husband who is a career military officer.

Date 32 — What is the mess that became your message?

Post-divorce, dating again, and a single mom, Carrie ended up settling for dating someone for two years who was simply "fine"; but he never really made the effort to integrate into Carrie's life with her family and friends, or to attend church with her on Sundays. She stayed in the relationship because it was "okay." She had resigned herself to a life that was void of true passion, simply choosing to stay safe.

At one Sunday's communion service, Carrie witnessed an older couple who both were unable to stand to make their way to the front of the church to receive communion and therefore they took communion together seated in their pews. The observation prompted her to realize what she wanted in a partner. She realized that she didn't want to settle for "just okay"; she wanted a life with someone who wanted to go to church with her — someone who would be her faithful companion at her side, even in old age. She had witnessed the beauty of a life of growing old together.

The message came loud and clear that Sunday morning: *Open yourself up to opportunity.*

Once Carrie received the message, she ended the two-year relationship and opened herself up to accept freely what life has in store. This is when life started to really happen for her. She watched amazing people and opportunities come into her life. Carrie shares this same message with her high-school-aged son: always be open to opportunity.

Now, Carrie is married to a man who sees the importance of being a part of her life — joining her on outings with friends and family, attending church with her, and embracing all that sharing a life together has to offer. Carrie is thrilled that she did not settle for just an okay life. She decided to live her best life.

The mess: Settling for an okay life because it feels safe.

The message: There is no need to accept a life that is simply okay. Open yourself up to opportunity, and trust that life will bring wonderful adventures and exceptional people your way.

Action step: Take a deep breath each day this week, and consciously open yourself up to the opportunities that the Universe will provide.

Journal

Today's date is:

This week, I'm going to let go of worrying, and open myself up to trusting the Universe. I am paying attention to the opportunities that come my way. For instance:

“Nothing is perfect.
Life is messy.”
— Anonymous

Chapter 33

Dee Dee's Story: Having Faith Gets Me Through the Storm

Born in Seattle, Washington
Fun fact: Dee Dee's favorite song is *Just Fine* by Mary J. Blige.

Out of all the friendships I've written about in this book, Dee Dee's and my friendship goes back the farthest. She and I grew up just two houses away from one another. We spent hours of our childhood playing outside, having sleepovers, sharing dinners, and even accompanying one another to church functions and school events — even though we attended different schools for most of our K–12 years. As children, we didn't see each other as Black or Asian — at least those labels didn't define us — we were simply friends. I'm sure we fought from time to time, but I honestly can't recall any childhood arguments that we may have had.

Date 33 — What is the mess that became your message?

While we spent a lot of time with each other during grade school, we spent less time together in middle school; and by the time we were in high school, our interaction was reduced to seeing each other only if we happened to be going in or out of our homes at the same time. Nevertheless, we never lost the genuine happiness we felt when seeing each other — even if it was just for a quick hello and a smile as we navigated life at two different schools with two different sets of friends. Both Dee Dee and I left our childhood homes for college.

Dee Dee had grown up in Seattle, a town she describes as a melting pot compared to other areas of the country. For instance, it is fairly common that in Seattle one might see a restaurant table with Black, Asian, and White people all seated together. So when she got to Southern University, an all-Black college located in Louisiana, she experienced culture shock — but in a good way. It was the first time she experienced classes taught by Black professors. She had had a few Black teachers here and there throughout K–12, but never a faculty of predominantly Black educators.

In Dee Dee's own words, she found herself "immersed in a community of Black people who wanted more in life, who wanted higher degrees, and good paying jobs." She found herself "in a Black community of peers who were not satisfied with where they were at; they had a contagious drive to achieve professional success."

Both of Dee Dee's grandparents were from Louisiana and had purposefully moved north for a better chance at life. Her granddad wasn't initially happy with her choice to move to Louisiana. He felt that after all he had done to get out of there, now she was taking a step backwards. But he eventually came around and ended up being very proud of Dee Dee and what she accomplished at Southern University.

In addition to reshaping her ideas of the world, college gave Dee Dee some significant challenges. She originally intended to major in architectural engineering; however, just before she began her freshman year, the major was dissolved, so her major then became architecture alone. After a year in the major, she found that she did not want to continue in architecture so she moved to civil engineering. Although successful, the classes were always a struggle, since civil engineering was not her ideal fit. Still, not wanting to change majors again, which would have extended her undergraduate career further, she stuck it out and graduated in five years with a BS in Civil Engineering. A few years later, she returned to school, receiving her MBA.

Just as in all other areas of Dee Dee's life, when she is challenged by a mess, her message is to let go of the control and give it all to God. She's a religious woman, with a strong belief in her Higher Power. Dee Dee told me, "I know that when I can't control a particular situation, or I start to feel overwhelmed, once I give it all to God, it always works out. It may not be what I expected or wanted, but it still works out."

Dee Dee's message is to let go of the need to control what you can't control, and give it all to your Higher Power. Trust in something greater than yourself. It will all work out.

The mess: Struggling to get through college when classes and the major you've chosen are not necessarily the right fit.

The message: There are things that I cannot control in life. Letting go of that urge to control and trusting in a Higher Power allows me to believe fully that despite my lack of control, it will all work out — and usually better than I imagined.

Action step: Let go of what you can't control today, and have faith in your Higher Power.

Journal

Today's date is:

Having faith means that I can let go of the fear of the things that I cannot control. For example:

Chapter 34

Carolyn's Story: Finding My Voice

Born in Bellingham, Washington

Fun fact: Carolyn has been in about thirty weddings as a bridesmaid, reader, and/or greeter. She is also a wedding officiant, having married six couples. She even officiated at the renewal of her parents' wedding vows, which took place at their fiftieth wedding anniversary celebration.

She enjoys writing original personalized readings for the ceremonies in which she participates.

Even though Seattle is big, it's often referred to as a small town. Everyone seems to know one another, or they can easily find out that they're separated by only a couple of degrees (using the Kevin Bacon scale of separation). Social media has made that even more true than ever. Carolyn happens to be one of those people I feel like I already knew even before I met her. I actually recall my first brief in-person introduction to her

— once at an outdoor summer pop-up party and then later at a jewelry shopping party at a mutual girlfriend's home. I always thought Carolyn was much younger than me. I even misidentified her and thought she was our mutual friend's twenty-something-year-old stepdaughter when I ran into her at a birthday party a couple of summers ago. She was actually forty-nine at the time. She not only has a youthful appearance, but her vibrant youthful light shines through from within.

Date 34 — What is the mess that became your message?

Just like me, Carolyn was always a checklist person. Throughout her life, she did everything in the order she was supposed to: She graduated from college, began her career, and got married — all before the age of thirty. The next step in what was expected of her was to have a child. As she progressed through her 30s, the pressure to have a child brought with it a lot of judgment and opinions from others, even from close friends. The decision about whether or not to have a child weighed heavily on her and turned into a very painful process. It was a mess.

To overcome the mess, Carolyn had to figure out what she really wanted for herself. At that point, having done everything in life that she was supposed to, to determine what she truly wanted for herself — and not what everyone else wanted her to do — took a lot of soul searching. Through this process, she realized that she didn't have to have her own child to care for a child. She saw that opportunities to nurture a child could come in many different ways. She could be a mentor, coach, and much more. She discovered that while figuring out what she wanted for herself, she found her own voice. She let go of others' judgments so that she could find what was best for her life.

Carolyn not only found her voice in the mess. She asked herself the question, "Why is my womanhood tied to the idea that you have to be a mother to feel worth?" She heard the message: "I am here to help and support others so that they can speak up and find their voice — now rather than later." She shares this story with the hope that it will help other women know that it is okay not to choose motherhood in your life journey. It is not a failure, and it does not diminish your worth; it is an acceptable personal choice.

A favorite saying that Carolyn shared with me is: "Life isn't about waiting for the storm to pass. It's about learning how to dance in the rain." I love this quote and plan to put it up in my office to remind myself that in the hard times, I can still move forward and find a way to do so with grace, happiness, and vitality.

Through the painful mess of self-discovery, Carolyn has found opportunity after opportunity to care for young people in so many ways other than through traditional motherhood. She is happily married to a man who has children, whom she adores. She is also a godmother and dotes on her godchild. And, she works with young adults in an organization whose mission is to empower them to move from minimum-wage jobs to meaningful careers. She is happy that she chose to live life on her own terms. Any motherly instinct is completely fulfilled by the younger people who are in her life whom she helps to guide into a better future.

The mess: Feeling pressure to have a child and tying it to your self-worth as a woman because of others' expectations.

The message: Through the process of figuring out what is right for me, I can find my voice, which means I can help and support others so they can speak up and find their own voice.

Action step: Think about the age that you began to find your voice. If you don't feel you're there yet, what is one step you can take today that will help you work towards that goal?

Journal

Todays date is:

When I examine my life, I see where I did things because they were expected of me. If I am being honest with myself, what I really want now is:

Queen

Queen

Chapter 35

Bunni's Story: Standing Up for Myself

Born in Houston, Texas
Fun fact: Bunni collects Jason Wu dolls and Ultra Limited Barbies.

Bunni and I met at a girlfriend's going-away party held at a Seattle restaurant. There were quite a few of us seated at a round booth. While the shape of the booth made it a little easier than a rectangular table would have been to talk to one another, it still wasn't too easy to interact with everyone at the table. We became Facebook friends after that initial gathering, and I later invited Bunni to a party which I was hosting at my home. I was thrilled when she came over, and we have been good friends ever since. We often comment that it feels like we've known each other for much longer than just the few years it has been.

Date 35 — What is the mess that became your message?

I enjoyed speaking with Bunni about her daughter, Ani — a young woman I loved from the moment I met her. Bunni describes

Ani as having always been a curious kid. Ani loved to explore. One day, when Ani was just two years of age, Bunni noticed a pea-size bump on the side of her daughter's neck.

From the moment she saw it, Bunni felt that something was not right. This was June 2001. After a number of doctor visits she was told by medical professionals that it would go away on its own. One doctor even suggested that the bump could be caused by the way Bunni was braiding or combing her daughter's hair. Then a visit to a physician at Seattle Children's Hospital resulted in a new diagnosis: Ani had swollen adenoids and tonsils. Still concerned about the bump and not fully buying the physician's belief that the bump was probably caused by drainage from the swollen adenoids and tonsils, Bunni persisted. To appease her concerns, the physician agreed to remove the bump during her daughter's scheduled tonsillectomy.

It was while waiting for her daughter to recover from the surgery that Bunni received the most difficult news, which dropped her to her knees: cancer. Her tiny two-year-old daughter was diagnosed with B-strain leukemia. Ani would endure twenty-seven months of chemotherapy — some of it administered orally, some through an IV, and even some through her tiny spine. Bunni learned from the doctors at Seattle Children's Hospital that it was the first time they had ever diagnosed leukemia based on a small bump on the side of the neck. Shortly thereafter, that specific symptom was added to the diagnostic protocol. Bunni is aware of at least two other children who were diagnosed early because the pea-sized bump is now part of the symptom list.

Ani survived. Once a Make-A-Wish kid, she has since grown up into a young adult who not only survived but also thrives.

When I asked Bunni what the message was that came from that terrible two-and-a-half-year mess, Bunni replied, "Make it happen." She went on to say, "Don't back down from something you believe in. Don't be intimidated by someone's position or title. Press on in your beliefs until you receive the answers you are looking for." She further advised, "Take control over your own health." Finally, Bunni added that she also learned that what Ani went through at age two was actually for a purpose: to save other children's lives.

The mess: Knowing something is wrong with your child's health and fighting to obtain the proper diagnosis and care for your child's medical needs.

The message: Stand up for yourself and make it happen when you know something is not right.

Action step: Take a stand this week for something you believe in. Whatever it takes — speak up, donate to a cause you believe in, and/or volunteer your time. Make your voice heard.

Journal

Today's date is:

I will stand up for myself in the following way:

"That's another fine mess
you've gotten me into."
— Anonymous

Chapter 36

Sarah's Story: Honoring Messages I Received from My Parents

Born in Hayward, Wisconsin
Fun fact: Sarah grew up log rolling in the lakes of Wisconsin.

Sarah and I met through mutual friends. I believe one of the first times we saw each other was at the bridal shower of a good friend's daughter. Sarah was seated in front of me and knew many more of the guests than I did. I remember her because she was friendly from day one. She is one of those people who, if she knows you don't know others, will make it a point to include you in the conversation. She is always very considerate of other people.

Date 36 — What is the mess that became your message?

Before we began discussing the mess we were going to talk about, Sarah declared plainly, "Life is messy." And boy, is she right. That is one thing I've learned from all of these conversations I'm having, is that it doesn't matter who you are — your race, politics, education level, economic level — life is messy for everyone.

The mess we discussed today was one that is very close to Sarah's heart. She lost both parents in the same year. Sarah's dad, while helping a friend, took a terrible fall, which broke his back. Although the fall did not immediately cause his death, he never fully recovered from surgery after surgery, and passed away not long afterwards.

If the loss of her beloved dad was not difficult enough, on the day of his burial, her mom was diagnosed with non-Hodgkin's lymphoma. She passed away just six months after the diagnosis, despite having one of the most commonly treatable forms of lymphoma.

Following her parents' deaths, Sarah was consumed with thoughts of her devastating loss. She recalls being at social events and despite her best efforts to make conversation, her mind would constantly drift back to the loss of her parents, still weighing heavily on her. She remembers attempting many times to socialize but feeling so incredibly burdened by the sorrow of her parents' deaths that it was hard for her to be her usual carefree self.

Not wanting the focus of conversation to be on her sadness, she started to feel that she was a burden on others. So that she wouldn't be a downer, she tried to speak about anything except the pain she was going through. She finally realized that she needed to talk to someone. She sought counseling to give her the ability to process her grief. She learned the importance of acknowledging when you need help, so that you can take responsibility to care for your own mental wellbeing.

Sarah is also reminded of the messages she received from her parents, which still stay with her today. She remembers one of her dad's visits from Wisconsin to Washington state. He witnessed some of Sarah's friendships, and commented on how great her friends were; he reminded her never to take them for granted. Her dad led by example, as he was social in nature, with great friends all around him. Her mom also left her a message — which Sarah received while cleaning out her mom's personal items. She found the following quote from American poet, memoirist, and civil rights activist Maya Angelou, which her mom kept both at home and in her office:

I've learned that people will forget what you said, people will forget what you did, but people will never forget how you made them feel.

Sarah has taken both messages from her father and mother to heart. It is no wonder that when I first met Sarah it was her kindness, friendliness, and considerate nature that drew me to her.

The mess: The horrible pain of both parents dying in the same year.

The message: Honor your parents by taking their messages to heart. Never take friends for granted, and remember that people will never forget how you made them feel.

Action step: Find a quote that embodies the spirit of your lost loved one. Write it down and keep it close to your heart.

Journal

Todays date is:

The messages Ive received from my parents that I never want to lose are:

"I'm a deeply feeling person in a messy world."

— Anonymous

Chapter 37

Cindy's Story: Loving My Child Through His Struggle with Addiction

Born in Youngstown, Ohio
Fun fact: While in the Air Force, Cindy took the last military flight to Iwo Jima before the US Coast Guard turned the island over to Japan.

Cindy and I met about twenty years ago. We worked together at a law office. I had just moved to a civil law practice after years as a prosecuting criminal attorney. I was fortunate to have Cindy as my paralegal, because she was not going to let me fail or drop the ball as I made the transition from criminal law to civil law. She was always prepared, never missing a beat. We worked well together, both of us schedule- and to-do-list-oriented. I love Cindy's dry wit, and her straightforward way of communicating.

Date 37 — What is the mess that became your message?

Cindy's two children both graduated from high school on time and moved on to college. Things were happening in the order that was expected. . .until her son's freshman year of college. While home for Spring Break, he received pain medication after having his wisdom teeth removed, and things went from zero to 100 — fast. Cindy can't say definitively if the pain medication was the catalyst for her son's battle with addiction, but it definitely seems to be the pivotal point in his story.

The next several years were filled with heartbreak, as her son cycled over and over again through drug use, living on the streets, detox, and a variety of rehab programs. While he kept in touch by phone, months would go by during which he was using drugs and living on the streets, and the family would not see him at all. Cindy realized through this painful process that she couldn't make him stop. He had to be the one to want to become clean and sober. Until he made that choice for himself, there was nothing she could do other than to be there if he ever reached out.

Her message received from this mess — which turned out to be a ten-year process — is:

1. Only the addict can choose to enter a rehab program for it to be successful. That choice can't be made by someone else.
2. This experience has given Cindy more compassion towards addicts and the homeless. When she sees people living on the streets, she recognizes that they have a mom, a dad — they are someone's son or daughter.
3. This experience has also given Cindy an understanding and compassion for anyone struggling with addiction and for those who have managed to become sober. Now, she reaches out to check in when she sees something difficult come up for them.

Fortunately, Cindy's son finally decided for himself that he wanted to get away from the drugs that were draining away his life. To this day, it is still work for him, but he utilizes a number of tools: counseling, a sponsor, and medication. He has also become a mentor. He is employed and recently became a first-time homeowner.

When we spoke of the mentorship that he is involved in, Cindy shared that one thing that drugs never took from her son was his caring nature. She remembers that even while on the streets, when he called for food, he asked that his parents bring some extra for someone he had met without a home who didn't have a family like he did. After listening to Cindy's story, I can't help but think that even on the streets, her son made a positive impact on the lives of others who were struggling just as he was.

When we ended our November virtual date, I told Cindy that she had inspired me to purchase socks to carry in my car to give to the homeless during this cold time of the year. She then shared with me a few other items that would be great to keep in a zip-lock bag for those we see on the streets: socks, Band-Aids, hand sanitizer, lotion, granola bars, candy, water, toothbrushes, toothpaste, hats, scarves, and gloves — things you can pick up at the Dollar Store. I'm grateful for my conversation with Cindy. She gave me a new perspective that I dearly needed: The homeless person I see living on the streets is someone's child.

Cindy and her husband are involved in Not One More Seattle/Tacoma (https://notonemoreseattle.org/) which is the local chapter of the national organization (https://www.notonemore.net/). The goal of the organization is to provide support to members of the local community who are struggling with addiction.

The mess: A son addicted to drugs and living on the streets, throwing his promising life away.

The message: You can offer to help people with a drug addiction, but it is not until they want to change for themselves that transformation can happen.

Action step: If you have children, or young people you mentor, let them know that you are here to guide them; but remember that you don't own them. Let them know that you will honor their life journey — that it is uniquely and wonderfully their own.

Journal

Todays date is:

This week, Im going to challenge myself to do at least one act of kindness towards a stranger who appears down on their luck, by doing the following:

Chapter 38

Lennaea's Story: Breaking the Cycle of Abuse

Born in Seattle, Washington
Fun fact: Lennaea was born at home, without the aid of modern medicine.

Lennaea and I met about fifteen years ago through a mutual friend. Tragically, the girlfriend who brought us together died in a car accident several years ago. Lennaea and I are blessed not only to have had that girlfriend in our life for the time that we did, but also to have met some other wonderful women through her.

From the moment I met Lennaea, she had me in stitches. Lennaea has a spirit about her that is contagiously fun. It only takes a short time after first meeting her to not only realize what a great sense of humor she has but also to see that she has the biggest heart. She is one of the most caring and compassionate people I have ever met. She is a true empath.

Date 38 — What is the mess that became your message?

Lennaea will be the first to tell you that her life has included a lot of monumental messes. Most were not of her own doing — they were curveballs that life threw her way. Looking at the number of messes in her life, Lennaea realizes that the catalyst for these messes stems from a very difficult and complicated childhood. She was raised in a home with a father who was terribly abusive. He had an alcohol and drug problem, and he was a narcissist. He mentally, physically, and emotionally abused Lennaea's mother and all the children in the family — especially her three older siblings.

Lennaea witnessed a lot of physical, verbal, mental, and substance abuse from a very young age by the people who were supposed to keep her safe and give her stability. Instead, she was neglected. She describes her childhood as a time with no expectations or support from her parents. They were so busy dealing with their own demons and survival needs that the children were left to find their own way.

While a few of my previous dates in this project described a struggle to find self-worth because everything had been tied to their parents' high expectations of them, Lennaea experienced the exact opposite. She grew up with the understanding that no one cared how well she did in school, whether or not she went to college, or any of the other types of expectations and hopes that parents usually bring to the table when they are trying to nurture better and brighter days for their children. There were no plans made for her future or for her siblings' future. While her dad was abusing drugs and alcohol, with volatile behavior at home, her mom was basically broken. The kids had to function as if they had no parents. Lennaea explained to me that when you grow up in a home like that, you grow up with constant anxiety, which can lead to depression, confusion, uncertainty, and self-doubt.

Lennaea is still processing the experiences of her childhood. She sees how her siblings have handled their trauma — many through substance abuse. She has had to carry on after her dear sister's suicide just a few years ago. Nevertheless, Lennaea has received many messages from the mess of her childhood. She shared several with me, along with tools that she has used to thrive rather than just survive.

One important tool comes from something that Lennaea's uncle shared with her. He looked at her one day and said, "Don't become what you despise." Those words have stayed with her.

Realizing that the abuse did not begin with her dad, but started in his family long before he was even born, Lennaea made the conscious decision not to be a victim of her childhood. She made an affirmative decision to break the cycle of abuse that had repeated itself for generations. She learned to trust her faith in God. Instead of anger and sadness, which used to dictate the way she walked through life, her message from the mess is that she always has a choice. And she has chosen to walk through life with grace, gratitude, integrity, and compassion.

Her biggest tools are faith and humor — her faith in God and her ability to find the humor in even the darkest situations. Surrounding herself with positive, uplifting people has been a huge factor in her healing. Lennaea also likes to be a positive influence on her two impressionable daughters. She has given them a much better childhood experience, and she intends to continue these efforts.

The mess: Growing up in an abusive home where you were left with zero support — no expectations to succeed and no foundation for growth.

The message: Don't become what you despise. Break the cycle. You always have a choice, in spite of the cards you have been dealt.

Action step: Do you see a pattern of abuse — or any type of negative pattern — that has continued in your family for generations? You can be the one who breaks that cycle, starting today.

Journal

Todays date is:

Hurts in my past do not define me. I can choose differently. I can break a negative cycle and start something new, which will have a positive impact on my life and carry on to the next generation. This week I will begin with the following:

Chapter 39

Tracy's Story: Letting What is Important to Me Guide Me

Born in Chicago, Illinois
Fun fact: The first time Tracy ever hiked was on a visit to Italy.

I met Tracy about twenty years ago. We were both practicing law in Pierce County, Washington, a county just south of Seattle. We were both members of the Pierce County Minority Bar Association. Unlike larger King County, where Seattle is located, Pierce County has so few attorneys of color that rather than having individual bars that focus on serving individual racial groups, which the larger county has available, Pierce County has one bar association that encompasses all attorneys of color.

Date 39 — What is the mess that became your message?

I had the honor of speaking with Tracy for our Zoom date on Veterans Day. Tracy served our country in the US Navy for eight years — four years on active duty and four years in the reserves.

Following college graduation, Tracy worked as a rehabilitative counselor with the state of Washington before entering law school.

It was during her first year of law school when life became messy. While fighting with the VA over benefits, starting law school, working, and experiencing marital difficulties with her first husband — a marriage headed for dissolution — Tracy learned that she was pregnant.

Tracy's beautiful daughter, Anna, arrived a few weeks early at the end of Tracy's first year of law school during finals week. Tracy recalls taking her Torts Final from bed — because, to add to the mess, she had been placed on full bed rest during her third trimester.

Looking back, Tracy says that she never gave herself the option to quit. She knew that she had to keep going because if she ever stopped moving forward, despite how hard some days were, she was afraid she'd stop completely.

The message from this mess came when Tracy interviewed with one of the most desired top five law firms in Seattle — a firm that paid one of the highest starting salaries for interns and first-year associates. The interview occurred during her second year of law school. She was told by one of the hiring partners that while the firm would love to offer her a position, they knew she had a baby. The hiring partner told her they needed to know where she placed her priorities.

That question made Tracy think. "I realized that my journey had to be around my daughter, so that she would receive what she needs. And I told myself: 'My time will come.'" Since that moment, and throughout Tracy's successful legal career, she has kept her commitment to prioritize the raising of her daughter as a guide for every decision.

Tracy realized that she could have it all. She could have a successful legal career without sacrificing being invested and present in her daughter's life. On a side note, Tracy's dedication to her daughter has paid off. At the time of our virtual date, Tracy's daughter was attending college on a full fellowship to the University of Illinois at Urbana-Champagne, pursuing her PhD in English.

The mess: Attending law school, a pregnancy that required full bed rest during the third trimester, and a divorce — all happening at once. Then, after that, receiving a dream job offer that forced a decision between work and family life.

The message: Deciding where your priorities lie and using that as a means to guide you through your decisions will never steer you wrong.

Action step: Take an honest look at what is taking most of your time this week. Does where you are spending your time align with your values?

Journal

Today's date is:

My top five life priorities are:

"Message starts with M-E-S-S."

— Anonymous

Chapter 40

Ronda's Story: Trusting That I Am Able

Born in Seattle, Washington

Fun fact: Ronda can write words backwards as quickly as she can write them forward. According to Ronda, when you hold her backwards writing up to the light, it is completely legible!

Ronda was my nurse for a minor surgery that I had years ago. While I don't make it a habit to befriend my medical surgical team, there is something that I loved about Ronda from the moment I met her. I had no make-up on, I was wearing a hospital gown, and my hair was in a hair net. Needless to say, that wasn't my usual first-impression look that I would have chosen. But Ronda doesn't see the outside of a person; she sees the inner beauty. That is part of what makes Ronda such an amazing nurse. From the moment I met her, I felt her kindness shine through, and conversation with her was easy. She not only made me feel comfortable before surgery, but she also made me feel beautiful just as I am.

Date 40 — What is the mess that became your message?

Ronda loves her parents dearly, but that love doesn't take away from the reality of how difficult some of her childhood was. She acknowledges and appreciates the growth that her parents have made during the years, especially following her older brother's suicide. She also acknowledges that there was a lot of mess that came from the pain that happened throughout her early life.

Ronda's stepdad, whom she simply calls "dad," was one of five kids, in a family that owned their own business. Worried that if his older brothers were drafted into the Vietnam War, the family business would suffer, he decided to volunteer to serve so that his brothers would not have to go. He was only eighteen years old then. Ronda doesn't know what her dad saw in Vietnam, but she knows it shaped who he became.

He had always been a hard worker. When he became a parent, he placed high expectations on his children. He and Ronda's mom wanted their kids to do better than they did. Unfortunately, they provided no guidance for them to do so. While her dad's intent was in the right place, his methods for implementing lessons often left his children feeling powerless.

Ronda shared an example of a painful childhood memory. She was a little girl, and her dad was driving her to a friend's birthday party. On the way to the party, her dad asked for street names and directions, all of which Ronda did not know. Ronda's dad's response was to take her home — and not only did he tell her she couldn't attend the party but he also grounded her until she was able to tell him the street names to the friend's house. Ronda was so young that she was not even able to leave their cul-de-sac let alone have the means to learn the street names.

This was before the internet so she had no viable age-appropriate tools that could have allowed her to even attempt to meet such a demand.

This was typical of Ronda's childhood experience. She was expected to do things without the proper guidance from her parents to achieve them. Her upbringing made her feel that she needed to be perfect, so she was always afraid she'd fail. This imposed perfectionism brought on constant anxiety because she usually didn't have the right tools readily available to succeed. This was a heavy weight for her to carry.

From the mess, Ronda learned that she had to figure out life on her own. She found her strength in her accomplishments, as she learned to accept things as they come and to give herself grace when some of her goals were reached more slowly than she had hoped. As she found her own way, she came to appreciate the pride that comes from making it on your own. As she learned to trust in her own abilities, she experienced the self-confidence that can be built over time.

The mess: Parents with unrealistic expectations, especially a father, who had high — often out of reach — expectations for his children but who offered no guidance.

The message: Trust in yourself. You have the power to accomplish so much on your own.

Action step: Teach yourself something new this week.

Journal

Today's date is:

This is an example of a time that I succeeded all on my own:

"My life is a beautiful mess
filled with wonderful messages."
— Anonymous

Chapter 41

Yolanda's Story: Escaping Credit-Card Debt

Born in Long Beach, California
Fun fact: Yolanda's favorite song is Tim McGraw's Spanish version of *Humble and Kind,* entitled *Nunca Te Olvides de Amar.*

I met Yolanda about twenty years ago when she and my cousin Ryan were engaged to wed. She has since become one of my favorite relatives. Yes, I admittedly have favorites. She is easy to talk to, and smart as all get out. I have so much respect for her. She is able to think quickly on her feet. She is one of those crafty individuals who can look at a Pinterest picture and execute the project perfectly. She is multi-talented. Yolanda has a great group of really close friends, and she is always available to support her friends and family. I imagine that in her circle of friends, she is the one that other friends go to for advice, because she approaches life with a healthy perspective. She seems to understand how things come together in the world, and what is important and what isn't. She is also quick to laugh and can find humor in every situation. Finally, in addition to being a great mother and wife, she has also made sure that her children were raised knowing both their Mexican and Japanese heritage.

Date 41 — What is the mess that became your message?

At age twenty-one, in her first year of marriage, while almost at the end of her third trimester with her first child, Yolanda was laid off from her job. As a young couple relying on two incomes, she and her husband found themselves suddenly a one-income family with a baby on the way. Yolanda describes the sudden change as challenging, and they had to quickly adapt to a new lifestyle.

After learning that they could manage on one income, even with a new addition to the family, they went a step further: They set the lofty goal of eliminating all credit-card debt. Yolanda purchased a nine-week financial program for $100 and used the structured plan as a framework towards becoming credit-card debt-free.

Together she and her husband made the commitment not only to live on one income but to become credit-card debt-free — and they accomplished this in only eighteen months. Yolanda laughs as she explains how hard it was. "It took sweat, tears, blood, and literally plasma" — as they donated plasma at one point to pay more of the debt down. Yolanda eventually began a business, but the money she earned continued to be flagged as "extra" for her family — for trips, savings, and such — as they kept to their commitment to live daily off of one income.

She has since brought her message of living debt-free to others, teaching what she has learned to the Spanish-speaking community in Skagit County, Washington, by volunteering to teach free finance classes. She emphasizes that it is always possible to work towards a debt-free life from wherever you are — even if you may have only an extra $10 a month to put towards knocking that debt down.

The mess: Suddenly moving from a two-income family to a one-income family while being strapped with credit-card debt and a baby on the way.

The message: Everyone can get out of credit-card debt if they stick to a plan.

Action step: Make a commitment today to become credit-card debt-free within the next five years.

Journal

Todays date is:

I am going to begin moving towards a life without credit-card debt today by:

"Life is meant for great adventure and close friends."

— Anonymous

Chapter 42

Roxanne's Story: Becoming Comfortable with Physical Displays of Affection

Born in Honolulu, Hawaii
Fun fact: Roxanne was crowned Miss Laoag City, representing the Philippines' sister city of Honolulu at that time. The opportunity allowed her to travel to Laoag City and other surrounding cities in the Philippines.

Roxanne and I met over twenty years ago. At the time, Roxanne was a law student and I was a fairly new attorney. We were both members of the Pierce County Minority Bar, an organization comprised of attorneys and law students of color, located in Tacoma, Washington. I think back to how much of life has happened for us both since that day we first met. Roxanne is now an Administrative Law Judge, married to her law-school boyfriend, and they have three lovely daughters. Her oldest daughter and both of my two children are now attending college.

Date 42 — What is the mess that became your message?

Roxanne remembers a time in grade school when she was with her mom, waiting outside of her classroom door for her parent–teacher conference to begin. She recalls witnessing her classmate and the classmate's mom who had just finished up with their conference ahead of her: They left the room and the mom paused to give Roxanne's classmate a big hug, telling her how proud she was.

The memory is still so vivid for Roxanne after all of these years because she was raised in a home where love was shown through hard work — not through any physical displays of affection. While growing up, she always knew she was loved by her parents. But she had never really thought about how being raised without physical displays of affection had affected her ability to communicate love as an adult.

It wasn't until after finishing law school, starting her career, getting married, and having her first child that she recognized that physical displays of affection — such as simple-hand holding with her husband — was something that didn't come naturally to her. She saw that her husband was much more comfortable showing affection than she was, and it was something that he valued. She learned that a relationship needs to include more than just a daily to-do list of laundry, dishes, and bills. Because she wanted their relationship to be nourished and growing, she took it upon herself to show affection. With this affirmation, she noticed that even a simple touch on her husband's back was enough to communicate her love during the day. Over time, she observed that by showing affection, she had become more open and more comfortable receiving affection.

During the COVID-19 pandemic, while working from home as an Administrative Law Judge, with her three daughters attending school remotely, Roxanne found that she needed to lock her home office door while court was in session. She had to do this because it was very common for her youngest daughter to walk in and jump on her lap to give her a big hug!

Roxanne has taken the mess of being raised without the luxury of living in a home where hugs are freely exchanged to acknowledging the message that showing affection is an important piece of nurturing a relationship. Because she got this message loud and clear, her daughters are being raised in a home where hugs are the norm.

The mess: Being raised in a home where physical displays of affection weren't a part of daily life, and therefore needing to learn how to be comfortable expressing affection as an adult.

The message: Practicing physical displays of affection at home with your partner is a wonderful way to strengthen relationships — and a delightful way of modeling love for your children.

Action step: Try a little PDA (public display of affection) today!

Journal

Today's date is:

I am going to show I care today by:

"Friendship is one of the sweetest joys of life."
— Anonymous

Chapter 43

Stacey's Story: Finding Perspective in the Mess

Born in Seattle, Washington
Fun fact: Stacey loves the color pink!

Stacey and I met at a mutual girlfriend's birthday celebration, when I was seated across the table from her. I found conversation easy from the moment I met her. We learned that our husbands were in the same fraternity in college, though at different times, as she and her husband are a few years younger than my husband and I.

A few months after Stacey and I met, while my husband and I were planning a home remodel, we learned that we had retained the same master builder that Stacey and her husband had hired. Without hesitation, she invited us to her home to see the stellar job they'd done with her house. And not only that; she wined and dined us. That's who Stacey is: She goes that extra mile to make the people in her life feel welcome and appreciated.

One of the charities that she supports is the Ronald McDonald House. Stacey is not someone who simply sends money without any reflection. She takes the time to package thoughtful gifts for the families who are staying at the Ronald McDonald House. It is obvious to anyone who sees her strikingly designed packages that a lot of love, thought, and care went into each and every one of them.

Date 43 — What is the mess that became your message?

At the beginning of our Zoom date, Stacey shared three statements that resonate with her, which have helped her through the hard stuff in life. These sayings have reminded her to put life's messes into perspective and they've helped to carry her through:

1. Everything happens for a reason. (*Have faith.*)
2. If there's a will, there's a way. (*Believe in yourself.*)
3. Things could always be worse. (*Get some perspective.*)

Stacey has had her fair share of messes in life. She told me about some heart-wrenching examples during our Zoom date.

Shortly after she graduated from college, Stacey was having no luck finding a job. During this time, her mom and dad were in a horrific car accident. Her mom was so badly injured that after a lengthy stay in the hospital, she was placed in a long-term rehabilitation facility before she could come home. Then upon returning home, her mom stayed bedridden for about a year.

Because Stacey had been unable to secure a job right after graduation, she was available to help take care of her mother — something she certainly would not have had the luxury of doing if she had found that brand-new job. The timing of her unemployment was perfect for what she, her mom, and her family needed.

Tragedy struck the family again, just a few years later. Stacey's dad was fifty-six years old when he collapsed at her father-in-law's home right before Christmas. Stacey applied CPR, but tragically, he did not recover. While her dad's death is still her most painful loss, she is so thankful that, of her siblings, she was the one who was there to attempt CPR. She thinks about her younger sister and fears that the heartbreaking experience of not being able to help in any way would have been absolutely devastating for her. She also appreciates that her father didn't have to suffer for a long time.

These are just a few examples of when Stacey's life has become messy. Because of her faith, her trust in her abilities to overcome whatever she puts her mind to, and her optimistic perspective on life, she has been able to navigate through all of life's messes — even the most painful ones.

The mess: Life's sudden tragedies can make things feel unbearable.

The message: Keeping the faith, believing in yourself, and finding perspective can help get you through life's inevitable messes.

Action step: If there is something in your life that feels particularly messy right now, think about what could be worse. Let that be a comfort to help you find the perspective that will reveal your choices and opportunities available, even right here in the mess.

Journal

Todays date is:

When things get bad, I find my strength by getting some perspective. For example:

“Friends are the family
you choose.”
— Anonymous

Chapter 44

Angela's Story: Living with Anxiety

Born in Edmonds, Washington

Fun fact: Angela was not only a high-school cheerleader but she became a cheerleader again at age forty — as a flyer with Cheer Seattle, which is a group of adult volunteer cheerleaders who perform to raise spirits, awareness, and funds for people living with life-challenging conditions.

Angela and I met years ago through our mutual girlfriend, Michelle. Angela and Michelle were both parents at the same small private Catholic grade school. We met when we were both invited to join in a girls' night out filled with dancing and lively socializing. At the time, I didn't realize that Angela's girls' nights out were far and few between. She was a single mom, working full-time, with two young grade-school-aged daughters — so that night was especially fun for her, a definite break from the daily grind.

Date 44 — What is the mess that became your message?

In my quest to speak with fifty-one women in order to write this book, I've had several friends — many whom I've known since my 20s — surprise me by sharing with me their daily struggle with anxiety. Each discussion has provided me with a better understanding of what living with anxiety feels like. This topic hits particularly close to my heart because I have a family member who suffers from living with an anxiety disorder, which is often accompanied by its sibling, depression. So, when someone shares with me their experience, I really do my best to absorb what they are sharing with me.

I was taken aback when Angela told me that her mess — which has been a lifetime mess — is living with anxiety and depression on a daily basis. I had always thought of Angela as my girlfriend who is so kind and even-tempered, she can get along with anyone. She loves to dance, and quite frankly, before our talk I'd thought of her as someone who is always happy. I never realized that she struggles daily with anxiety and depression.

Angela described what living with daily anxiety and depression since childhood feels like. She went on to say that it was even harder in her teenage years and during college. The anxiety was so great in college that she left school before completing her degree, despite the fact that she was very close to finishing.

Now, as an adult, she has learned from her experiences, and so she is constantly striving to effectively use the tools that work for her to manage her anxiety and depression. She has continually sought to find the messages from her messes. She notes that often times, it could be exhausting — but this struggle has also made her someone who is able to sense the pain in others. The life-long struggle with anxiety and depression has brought Angela wisdom that comes from learning to dig deep and to spend time on self-reflection.

Angela described for me that anxiety can sometimes feel like she is living life in quicksand while everyone else seems to be zooming by easily. This visual was very powerful for me and helped me gain a greater understanding of what it feels like to live with an anxiety disorder. Angela now accepts anxiety and depression as a part of who she is. She is okay with it, no longer comparing herself to others. Instead, she accepts herself fully just as she is.

The mess: Living with daily anxiety and depression.

The message: Accept yourself just as you are.

Action step: This week, whenever you find yourself feeling anxious, pause for a few moments, close your eyes, and take five deep belly breaths to try to calm and center yourself. Give yourself the gift of time for relaxation and self-reflection.

Journal

Todays date is:

I will work on alleviating anxiety and/or depression by doing things I know will help me to create a better lifestyle — such as regular exercise, eating healthy food, getting enough sleep, meditating, limiting caffeine and alcohol, and so on. Today, I choose:

"Never let your best friends get lonely. . .keep disturbing them."
— Anonymous

Chapter 45

Tracie's Story: Fighting for My Son's Life

Born in Seattle, Washington
Fun fact: Tracie's favorite song is
Independent Women by Destiny's Child.

Tracie and I met through her sister, Dana, who wrote the Foreword for this book. I've told Tracie that when we met, she greeted me with such warmth, that it made me instantly feel as if we had been friends forever. From that moment, I knew that the way I felt when she greeted me is the way I want people to feel when they meet me. Since that first meeting, I've changed the way I greet people. I now greet new friends with the extra warmth that I learned from Tracie. She gave me this gift, which now sets the foundation for my new friendships. It seems so simple, but it really is a lesson that has changed my relationships and transformed my life.

Date 45 — What is the mess that became your message?

Tracie shared two big life messes that have become her messages. These are messes that have contributed to shaping who Tracie is today. She has become an inspirational public figure, a speaker, an author, and for many women a beacon of hope. She truly is a fighter, a survivor, and a thriver.

The first mess that Tracie shared with me is told movingly in her book entitled *Incompatible with Nature: Against the Odds: A Parent's Memoir of Congenital Heart Disease.*

While on a college Spring Break trip to Mexico, Tracie met a man from Germany. Despite the language barrier and distance, she fell head over heels in love. After a whirlwind romance and long-distance dating — which all happened well before email or texting, at a time when international phone calls cost an arm and a leg — he asked her to marry him, and she said *Yes!* With only knowledge of a few German words, Tracie packed up, left the security of her friends and family, and moved to Germany to start a new life.

As many young couples are, she and her husband were joyous when they found out they were expecting a child. Tracie soon gave birth to their only child, a beautiful baby boy. He was perfect. But before long they learned that their darling boy had been born with just half of his heart. I can only imagine their tremendous fear and heartbreak when they heard the news. In her poignantly written book, Tracie describes the harrowing journey of the fight to save her son's life.

Being a first-time mom is always a mess; moving away from family and friends to live in a foreign country is a mess; being unable to speak the language of the country that is now your home is certainly a mess. Now add the fact that you have a child born with such a serious health condition that you are constantly fighting to obtain the medical care that will save him — and the word *mess* doesn't even adequately describe your life.

Fighting for her child's medical care was not the only mess that Tracie was dealt during this time in her life. Her marriage became increasingly unhealthy. While her son's health was her primary focus, she eventually had to come to terms with her destructive marriage. Again, without family nearby to support her, and still living in Germany, she had to dig deep to find the courage and strength to make it on her own. She had to trust her ability to survive. Her husband was the family breadwinner and she was a stay-at-home mom. Leaving the marriage, going out on her own in her adopted country, and navigating a court system that was foreign to her, was not at all easy. She recalls that each morning, she woke up and willed herself to move: "Get up and get on it!" Tracie would say to herself. And that is exactly what she did.

There are three messages Tracie shared with me that these big life messes have taught her:

1. Get up and get on it! (*Be your own advocate.*)
2. Recognize your own strength. (*You are stronger than you think.*)
3. Failure is not an option. (*Tracie believes that when you have this attitude, you will keep moving forward and you will get to the other side.*)

The mess: Fighting for your son's medical care and making it on your own in a country and culture far from home.

The message: You are stronger than you may think, so get up and get on it, because failure is not an option.

Action step: You have only one life to live. Live it to the fullest. What do you dream of doing? Set a goal, commit to it, and never give up.

Journal

Todays date is:

I can do anything I set my mind to. Today I will:

Chapter 46

Kirsten's Story: Doing Something Every Day That Scares Me

Born in Minneapolis, Minnesota

Fun fact: Kristen's favorite quote is from Anaïs Nin: "And then the day came, when the risk to remain tight in a bud was more painful than the risk it took to blossom."

Kirsten and I met just a couple of years ago at a girlfriend's house. Our girlfriend invited several women to her home — women who had inspired her and made a difference in her life — and both Kirsten and I were fortunate to be included in that group of remarkable women. The more I get to know Kirsten, the more I understand our mutual girlfriend's sentiment. Kirsten is truly someone who is here to make a positive difference in the world.

Date 46 — What is the mess that became your message?

During a four-month-long period of time, Kirsten's world imploded. When her oldest son left home to attend college, his move hit her hard. While she was redefining her identity as a mom with a son now living away from home, her husband — whom she had been married to for twenty-three years of the thirty years they had been together, told her that he was gay.

While some couples are able to stay married in such a situation, Kirsten knew that their marriage was over. The marriage was no longer right for either of them. While trying to wrap her head around what her new future was going to look like, she received the call that no parent wants to receive. Kirsten's middle son — who was sixteen at the time — was involved in a bad car accident. He has since recovered remarkably, but at the time of the accident his brain injury was so significant that his future was uncertain.

During those four months, and all the rest of that year, Kirsten would hear herself tell people, "I'm such a mess. And this isn't me."

She found that after being with her husband for her entire adult life, she was afraid to be single. For awhile, she was simply surviving each day, going through the motions, making sure her kids were okay. Her life was deconstructing, as they were selling their house and figuring out how to divide their lives. It even came down to the question, "Who gets the kids' school art?"

Through that process, she realized that she needed to do more than just survive. She needed to be a model for her kids so that they would know that everything was going to be okay. She needed to show them hope amidst the uncertainty.

Many fears cropped up for Kirsten — her life that had been so suddenly shaken. One of the things that helped her get through her fear of being alone and much more was a book entitled *Do One Thing Every Day That Scares You,* by Robie Rogge and Dian G. Smith. For a whole year, Kirsten actually did it: Every day, she did one thing that scared her. For example, she got out of her comfort zone and initiated a conversation with a stranger at the end of a yoga class; she went paragliding; she embarked on a solo international trip; she took a hip-hop class (challenging herself to stand in the front row of the class); she took helicopter flight lessons; and she ventured on her own to movies, restaurants, musicals, and museums. All of these things were completely out of her comfort zone, but she did it. And she found that when you successfully face smaller fears, you gain confidence in your ability and realize how strong you are. "Each time it becomes easier and easier so that when the bigger fears come along, you know that you can tackle them."

I learned a lot from my conversation with Kirsten, as she told me about the messages that she received — and still receives — from those initial four months of upheaval. She shared with me that it is important to give yourself grace. A wise friend shared with her that when you are healing from trauma, it is expected that sometimes you might take a step backward in your healing. But remember, when you take that step backward, you aren't falling all the way back to square one. The old adage of "two steps forward, one step back" carries some truth. "Life is not always linear, so taking a step back doesn't mean you're going back to square one."

Kirsten not only survived this time of turmoil, but she has used her experience to help others by creating an amazing podcast, *An Unexpected Launch*. She is a gifted interviewer, guiding her guests as they share their stories of how they forged through life's unexpected challenges. Her podcast inspires and provides others with the strength and knowledge that they can make it through whatever life throws their way.

The mess: Your entire life and your expected future basically changing overnight.

The message: Have patience with yourself and give yourself grace for the journey. Face your fears at your own pace — knowing that each time you conquer a fear, the next one can feel a little less scary.

Action step: Make a list of up to ten things that scare you. Now make a plan to take one small step that you can do to conquer each fear.

Journal

Todays date is:

Today, I am going to challenge myself by facing just this one fear of mine by doing the following:

Chapter 47

Theresa's Story: Navigating Young Adulthood Without Parents to Guide Me

Born in Seattle, Washington

Fun fact: Theresa has always been an animal lover. She and her best friend have rescued many stray dogs and cats over the years, and she and her husband have raised three fur babies of their own.

Theresa and I grew up in the same neighborhood, and one of her best childhood friends was also a good childhood friend of mine. We remember both of us being at some of the same birthday parties when we were kids. We've been fortunate to reconnect as adults through social media. And, with Theresa, as it often is with people who grew up in the same neighborhood as you, conversation is instantly easy.

Date 47 — What is the mess that became your message?

Theresa did not have the luxury that most people do — to have her parents by her side as she navigated adulthood. Theresa's mom died when Theresa was only seventeen years old. During Theresa's junior year of high school, her mother was given a cancer diagnosis. Just a few days after that, she was taken to the hospital for a hysterectomy to remove the cancerous growth. Her mom never left the hospital, but died just eighteen days later due to complications related to the surgery. While her mom's sudden death was hard to process at only seventeen — an age that is already confusing enough — at least Theresa still had her dad.

Theresa describes her dad as her rock. When she spoke of him on our virtual date, I saw that she grappled to find adjectives to describe him because words alone didn't seem sufficient to convey the admiration and love she had for her dad. Theresa recalls that it was important for her to "be a good kid and to do everything right." Looking back, she realizes that her motivation came from her desire to make her father happy and proud.

Theresa married young. She remembers being on her honeymoon, sitting on the beach next to her new husband and wondering, "What am I doing?" While her marriage was not happy, things really came crashing down when her father died. Theresa was only twenty-five years old, and her dad was only sixty-three when he died of heart failure.

Soon after her dad passed, she divorced her husband. In her mid-20s, without either parent and recently divorced, Theresa started down a rough road, where her grief manifested into many unwise choices. She spent a year feeling really lost. Fortunately, going through that difficult year brought a lot of understanding and gave her the ability to redefine who she was as an adult. Not only that, but she also met the love of her life, a man with whom she has made a lovely family and home.

Theresa shared three messages she has received from the mess of losing both her parents at such a young age:

1. Let go of the things that hurt you, and hold on to the special memories.
2. If you've lost your parents, stay close to the people who loved your parents like you did.
3. If you have the opportunity to take care of your aging parents, remember that it is a privilege.

The mess: Being a young adult without parents to guide you.

The message: It's a privilege to take care of aging parents who raised you, and to have mentors to help guide you.

Action step: Call, email, or text someone today to let them know how much they mean to you.

Journal

Todays date is:

I am going to show my parents and/or my guardians or mentors that I appreciate them by doing the following:

"Best friends — they know
how crazy you are and still
choose to be seen with
you in public."
— Anonymous

Chapter 48

Simone's Story: Growing Up Different

Born in San Andres, Colombia
Fun fact: Simone is an artist and creator — talents that she inherited from her mom.

For seven years in a row, I hosted a large Cookie Exchange Party at my home on the first Saturday morning of December. The Cookie Exchange tradition grew from about twenty-five women to ninety women, as it expanded in size each year. At many of these cookie exchanges, especially early on when the party wasn't quite so big, I had the space in my home that made it possible for the luxury of allowing friends to invite their friends to join the party. One year, Simone was invited by a mutual friend. I don't remember which friend invited her; but we have since discovered that we have many friends in common.

Date 48 — What is the mess that became your message?

As children, and even sometimes as adults, all we want is to feel like we fit in. Imagine growing up in the 1970s when the nuclear family — the ideal TV family — consisted of a mom, a dad, and home-cooked evening dinners together. . .and then there was *your* family.

Simone's mess was "growing up different." She was raised by a single mom who was an artist with a free-spirited lifestyle. Her mother loved getting together with her artist friends, who were similar in spirit — not the conservative crowd of stay-at-home moms that Simone envisioned her friends' moms were hanging out with. Also, being of mixed race, Simone remembers always feeling like she was different, and that her home life was different from that of other kids. She grew up understanding that while she knew her mom always supported her, because she was a single working mom, she wasn't ever going to be available in the same way that many of her friends' stay-at-home moms were.

Simone was born on a small island in South America. She told me a story that her mom had shared with her. One day, she and her mom were walking home from the grocery store. Simone had just learned how to walk. On their walk home, there was a torrential rain. Simone had sandals on, and each step was a fight against the sinking mud. Her mom remembers this moment, because with her hands full of groceries, she was unable to pick up her struggling toddler. Her mother recollects watching Simone carefully fight against the mud, placing one foot in front of the other. Even though Simone had just learned to walk, her mom recalls, she watched her daughter quietly make it on her own.

This story her mother shared is a fitting example that symbolizes what Simone learned from her mess. She learned to be independent, to be a problem-solver, and to be a woman who values community. She is a staunch advocate for children who need support — and she is someone who recognizes where help is needed, especially where children are concerned. She has been a consistent volunteer throughout her daughters' schooling, especially the younger K–5 years — letting other mothers who weren't able to volunteer know that she would be available to help their children, if needed.

Simone took her sometimes very painful mess of growing up feeling like she was different, and made what she learned as a child into one of her greatest strengths as an adult. She is someone who notices others who may be struggling, and jumps in to be that mom, that friend, that sister.

The mess: Feeling like you don't fit in anywhere.

The message: Your childhood struggles can become one of your greatest gifts to children whom you may be uniquely able to understand and support as an adult.

Action step: Do something this week to help someone younger than you.

Journal

Todays date is:

I can use what Ive learned from my childhood messes as my guide to supporting the next generation, in the following ways:

"Sometimes, being silly with a friend is the best therapy."
— Anonymous

Chapter 49

Tiffani's Story: Acknowledging My Adoption Trauma

Born in Seoul, Korea
Fun fact: Tiffani's adoptive parents were both very fair-skinned, both six feet tall, and both very Southern!

Tiffani and I share a special bond that stems from our life experiences. We were both abandoned by our birth families in South Korea, and we were later adopted through the same adoption agency in the 1970s. This was at a time when interracial and international adoptions were uncommon, and Korea was the first country to export their orphaned children for adoption. Speaking with Tiffani during our Zoom date was the first time I had ever spoken to another Korean adoptee about our adoption experiences.

Date 49 — What is the mess that became your message?

It is the "luck of the draw" what family you will end up with when you're adopted — especially back in the 1970s when international adoption wasn't the somewhat well-oiled machine that it is today. Tiffani was adopted at three and a half years of age, when she was taken from South Korea to rural Huntsville, Alabama, USA. Tiffani describes her adoptive family as absolutely loving. Her dad was in law enforcement as a state trooper, and her mom was a nurse. She describes her sister, who was three and a half years older (a biological child of her parents), as an "angel," and they were very close. Tragically, all three passed away. Her sister died in a fatal drunk driving accident in 1986, and both parents died of cancer in 2014.

Tiffani has survived her entire adoptive family. She now resides with the apple of her eye, her teenage daughter, Malia.

Early in 2020, due to the pandemic, Tiffani was furloughed for seven months from her job. This layoff turned out to be a blessing, giving her time to reflect back on her life. The time off work forced her to "be quiet" to take an honest look at herself. Through this process of introspection, she got involved with a non-profit group for transracial and international adoptees. The mission of the group is to eliminate transracial and international adoptee suicide through mental health advocacy and support.

I loved the open and honest discussion I had with Tiffani that day. Like me, Tiffani did not grow up with other adoptees, and we both went through a significant period of our life rejecting our Korean roots — not wanting to have anything to do with other Korean people or Korean adoptees. However, as we have grown older, we've realized that there is a benefit to connecting with those who share a similar history. As Tiffani explained to me, there are a lot of adoption-related issues that many adoptees share, which are often overlooked. When adoptees struggle with mental health, they can often be misdiagnosed and/or treated only considering the period of time from the adoption forward — with the original adoption trauma and the separation from the biological family ignored.

Tiffani and I discussed the trauma of adoption: being pulled from one's birth family, being placed into a new family, being taken away from one's birth country and culture, and being raised in a family where no one looks like you. As Tiffani said, for many interracial adoptees, including her own experience growing up in rural Alabama, "it is like living in a fun house — where everyone around you is White, and then you look at a mirror and you look like a monster. Your hair is different, your eyes are different, your skin is different, and you don't fit in anywhere, even at home."

The message Tiffani received from the mess of experiencing and then identifying her own adoption trauma is that she is here to educate and empower transracial and international adoptees and their families. She encourages them to acknowledge and recognize the trauma so that tools can be provided for adoptees to navigate their identity, appreciate their value, and learn to trust.

As she pointed out, these tools weren't available for our generation of adoptees, so we had to figure it out for ourselves, often in isolation. It is her hope and her mission that future generations of transracial adoptees will have the tools, the resources, and the support to feel empowered and educated as they travel through life. She wants all transracial adoptees to be able to understand our early trauma, while also celebrating at the same time the beauty of adoption, embracing the differences that may exist between the adoptee and the adoptive family.

The mess: Unaddressed trauma stemming from adoption.

The message: Balance the struggles, including recognizing the adoption trauma of a child separated from their birth family. At the same time, celebrate the beauty of a family created through adoption.

Action step: Identify any of your past traumas that are ready to be worked on this year. Take affirmative steps to seek the help you need.

Journal

Todays date is:

While I am not going to dwell on my childhood trauma, I will acknowledge it; and, if needed, I will seek the tools and resources to help me navigate through my childhood experience for a better adult life. First, I will:

Chapter 50

Rachel's Story: Knowing I Can Get Through Any Mess

Born in Seattle, Washington
Fun fact: She is "very left-handed" and
she loves George Michael's music.

Rachel and I initially met through social media. We have many mutual friends — real-life in-person friends. Given the large number of mutual friends we have, and since both of us are social butterflies, meeting in person at some point was simply inevitable. Rachel happens to be one of those people who — whether you meet online, on the phone, or in person — makes you almost instantly feel like you've been friends for years. She has a natural ease about her. She can not only talk with anyone, she also makes everyone she talks to feel comfortable right away.

Date 50 — What is the mess that became your message?

Rachel's mess was her most painful loss. Rachel's mom was fifty-nine years old when she received a diagnosis of Stage 2b triple-negative breast cancer. In just a three-month period of time, her mom's cancer metastasized, changing from a Stage 2b diagnosis to a devastating Stage 4 diagnosis. Rachel's mom passed away just a couple of weeks following her sixtieth birthday. Rachel was thirty-five when she lost her mom. Rachel's mom's fight against cancer included various chemo drugs, none of which worked on the type of cancer her mom had. Being by her mom's side and watching her fight and ultimately lose her battle against cancer was the most painful and emotion-filled year Rachel had ever experienced.

Only ten to fifteen percent of breast cancer diagnoses are triple negative. It is a very aggressive form of cancer. While some recent research has located possible new treatments that look cautiously promising, such possibilities were not available when Rachel's mother was diagnosed. A triple-negative breast cancer finding is still a very dire diagnosis to receive.

Rachel took that mess, and made it her message. Her mom's death gave her clarity. The pain and grief Rachel had endured granted her the strength to get through her other life messes. She recognized that if she could survive something that heart-wrenching, then she could survive anything.

Soon she came to the realization that she had the strength to end a fourteen-year marriage that had not been good for many years. The divorce itself was messy — not a simple or amicable process. Because it was contentious, it took about a year to complete. When things got tough, Rachel held to her strong mindset: Because she knew she had made it through the most painful experience in her life with her mom's illness and death, there was nothing she could not handle. She knew she could and would survive anything.

The mess: A daughter's most painful loss — the loss of her beloved mother to cancer.

The message: Recognize the strength that you've developed by surviving your most painful mess, and you'll see that you have the ability to make it through anything.

Action step: Write down the top three times in your life when you're proud of the strength you showed.

Journal

Todays date is:

My strength was revealed to me when I survived the struggle and pain of ____________________.

This reminds me that when a new mess comes along, I'll be up to the task. I can survive anything, because I have the following strengths and resources:

"Good friends don't let you do stupid things. . .alone."

— Anonymous

Chapter 51

Connie's Story: Accepting that I'm Imperfectly Perfect

Born in Eureka, California
Fun fact: Connie loves karaoke, and her favorite karaoke song is *Blue Bayou* by Linda Ronstadt.

Connie was my children's Montessori preschool teacher. Both of my children are now in college, so that tells you how long I've known Connie. For many years, we lived in the same area of Seattle and because of that, we have many mutual friends. I've since moved out of the area but enjoy keeping in touch with Connie through social media.

Date 51 — What is the mess that became your message?

When we began our Zoom date, Connie told me that what she was going to share felt vulnerable to her. She and I are about the same age and the mess she was about to describe is one that I can relate to — something many of us experience and struggle with.

Connie opened up about the mental and emotional struggle that comes from aging. She shared the negative self-talk that she fell into, in particular as it related to body image. Looking back at her life, Connie realizes that she was fortunate to be an incredibly confident teenager and young adult. She was an accomplished and gifted athlete who participated in a sport every season. She always had friends and she never worried about not fitting in. She never experienced those uncomfortable awkward teenage years that so many of us remember.

Then, adulthood came. She married and had two children, and her focus was now on her family. With the life changes — having children, and moving into her 30s and 40s, as it does for us all — her body changed. For the first time in her life, she felt self-conscious in her body. She was not happy in her own skin, always comparing herself to the athlete she once was. She found herself not fully accepting who she was anymore. For years, she carried around the burden of a lot of heavy negative self-judgment.

After years of fighting to regain the body she'd once had back in college and placing much of her own self-worth on whether or not she achieved her weight and strength goals, she started to learn the art of grace.

The message from the mess came in the form of learning how to be kind to herself. She focuses on all the good that her body can do. This message really hit home for her when her best friend was diagnosed with breast cancer, and she walked that journey alongside her. Realizing that while she enjoys the feeling of being fit and getting regular exercise, she does not have to be perfect. Because she practices grace, Connie has been able to accept who she is. In times when she is at her fittest, as well as when the scale isn't cooperating, she loves herself with kindness and full acceptance.

And what a good note to end on with these fifty-one dates with friends — with the powerful message simply to be kind to ourselves. Let's celebrate how "imperfectly perfect" we all are!

The mess: Negative self-talk — in particular, a negative body image.

The message: You are imperfectly perfect.

Action step: Stand naked in front of a full-length mirror and appreciate all the amazing things that your magnificent body has done.

Journal

Today's date is:

I give myself the gift of grace. Every time I recognize any negative self-talk, I will counteract it with these kind and loving thoughts for myself:

"Life is better with friends."

— Anonymous

Chapter 52

Author's Story: Sharing My Own Mess-to-Message Experience

Born in Seoul, Korea

Fun fact: In law school, I studied 3-5 subjects at a time. I would lay 3-5 class casebooks open on my circular kitchen table and proceed to read one paragraph of the first book, move to the next book to read one paragraph of that book, and so on — until I finished all of my reading assignments for the day. During that same time, which was the early to mid-90s, I made meals using cookbooks in the order they were written, page by page. My cookbook method was great for variety but became challenging when it came to the drink or dessert sections; but because I'm wired to be a rule-follower, even if it is my own quirky rules that I'm following, I did not deviate from my method — and often times it was at least a full week of desserts, if not longer!

Like many of us, I have had so many life messes, it is hard for me to choose just one to share in this final chapter. During this project, I heard a similar sentiment from a good number of the women I spoke to: "How do I pick just one? My whole life has been messy!"

For this final chapter, I will begin with what I perceive as my initial mess:

Day one of my life. One big mess.

Abandoned approximately two months after birth, found in a cardboard box in a parking lot in Seoul, Korea in 1970 without any identifying information — no name, no birth date — my start in life was a big mess.

My story began long before I was born. After seeing a documentary film about GI babies of the Korean War who were left in Korea, Harry and Bertha Holt, an Oregon couple with six biological children, decided they would adopt some of these children who needed families. Harry began preparations to travel to Korea, and Bertha asked a friend how to go about adopting children from another country. Learning that it would be possible only if both houses of Congress passed a law allowing it, Bertha Holt decided to push for just such a law.

Two months later, the "Holt Bill" was passed, and in October 1955, Harry Holt and eight children from Korea arrived at the Portland International Airport. The resulting publicity stirred interest among many families in the United States. The Holts set about helping others to adopt, which led to the creation of the Holt International Adoption Agency. While I am not a direct product of the Korean War, I am considered part of the first generation of international and transracial adoptees.

I grew up before the internet, before social media, before the modern-day tools that are available now to connect adoptees. Today a curious child or teen can easily research and read about the adoption experience of other adoptees. I grew up without knowing any other Korean adoptees or Korean people.

While most Asian adoptees are adopted into White families, I was adopted by an Asian-American couple, which today is still very rare. My parents were "older" parents — my dad was forty-eight, and my mother was forty-one when they adopted me. These ages would not be considered particularly old now, but back in the 1970s, these were the ages of my childhood friends' grandparents.

My adoptive parents are both of Japanese-American descent. Because they were born and raised on the West Coast of the US, they and their families were interned during World War II. My mom's family, from Bainbridge Island, Washington, was one of the first to be interned. If you happen to visit any Japanese-American internment museum, a photo of her family being led to trains headed for an internment camp will undoubtedly be found on the museum wall.

While my dad and I were very close, I struggled with my relationship with my mom. I am not fond of the phrase *she did the best she could with what she had,* but in this case I think it fits. I didn't meet my mom's expectations, and somehow we failed to form a mother–daughter bond. I believe that some of the feelings of not being accepted by my adoptive mom — never forming that all-important mother–daughter bond — contributed heavily to my insecurity and the self-destructive behavior that I exhibited during my teenage and early adult years.

During my high-school years, I decided that the only person besides my dad that I could count on was me. I changed high schools several times, attending four different high schools in four years. I was lonely. I had unsatisfying relationships, because I always put myself first in the relationships that I did have. In other words, I found myself often hurting others, before they could hurt me. My insecurities caused me to make poor life choices when it came to relationships with my girlfriends and with young men through my teens and early 20s. I did not have a female role model, so my female friendships were not strong. I was living in constant fight-or-flight mode.

Losing my dad a month after I turned thirty-two was a pivotal time in my life. My worst fear came true when I got that call at about 5:30 in the morning from my mom. My dad had collapsed in the bedroom and paramedics were on the way. She was very distraught on the phone. She was attempting CPR. My husband and I dropped what we were doing and jumped in the car. He drove — he didn't want me to drive in my shocked state.

We pulled up to my parents' home which was about thirty minutes away. My parents' home sat on a corner lot and when we pulled up, bright ambulance and police car lights were framing the house, lighting up the dark sky. The awful image of pulling up to the house and seeing so many flashing lights will forever be embedded in my mind's eye. I ran into the house. I was asked by the first responders at the scene if I wanted to see him, but he was already gone. My dad had died before I arrived. I declined. I didn't want my last image of him to be of his death. I wanted my last memory of him to be his smiling face and all the good talks we'd had together. He died on January 25, 2001, which coincidentally was my mom's 72nd birthday.

I became a mother soon after my dad died. It was just four and a half months later, in May 2001, that my husband and I received notice that our own two-year adoption journey was finally culminating in a match: We received a picture of our baby girl who was waiting for us in China. One of the biggest heartaches in my life is that I never got the chance to witness the joy that would have come from watching my dad interact with my children.

At the time of the adoption referral, we had just put both our home and my mother's home on the market. It was a knee-jerk reaction on my part to look for a place with a mother-in-law apartment so that my mom could live with us. I was trying to take care of all the things and people that I thought my dad would have wanted me to care for. I was trying my best to do good by him. While we thought our house had sold right before we left for China in early June of 2001 — moving all of our belongings into storage — we learned just days before we were due to fly out that the sale had fallen through. We were a young couple and needed that home sale to purchase our second home.

We left for China to pick up our daughter with no home of our own to come back to. We quickly set up house in my mother's small home, with a make-shift nursery and my husband and me sleeping in my childhood room.

Two weeks after we returned from China, we learned that not only were we first-time parents of our precious daughter, but I was also pregnant. I was practicing law at the time as a defense attorney for a large national insurance company. I had to cut my maternity leave in half when we learned that I was pregnant, because a second maternity leave was now planned for later the same year. Our son was born eight months later.

Fortunately, by the time my son was born, we were in a new home, with my mom living in her own part of the house. The multi-generational living arrangement eventually fell apart, with my mom moving into a retirement community — which made both my mother and me much happier.

I think we both learned that we could not feign a bond simply because the person whom we'd both loved, my dad, had died. I have since learned to be okay with the relationship I have with my mom. While I no longer seek that bond with her that I once yearned for, I also no longer harbor the anger and resentment towards her that I used to carry around with me. I realize that I can accept who she is as she is, and appreciate her place in my life.

It is hard for me to pinpoint one turning point in my life, the point where I learned to trust people and realize that I needed true friendships. I do know that the process began when I decided to work on letting go of the fear of judgment. Being controlled by the fear of judgment was my biggest life-long mess. The fear of judgment dictated my actions and choices in my young adult life. It stopped me from fully living, from fully embracing life, and from welcoming people into my life. Once I was able to let go of this fear, I was able to see the connection I had with everyone around me and I could relate on a much deeper level.

I learned that fear is often based on something that hasn't even happened and may never happen. Fear prevents me from living in the present.

The experience of asking my friends *What is the mess that became your message?* has helped me to be more connected to my girlfriends than ever before. None of us is perfect. We all create messes, or we are thrown into messes that are not of our own choosing. Either way, we have to deal with life's messes all the time. But living through these messes, we find our messages: We learn and grow, and then we are equipped to be here to support each other and to learn from one another.

These conversations not only deepened my friendships but they have allowed me to recognize how connected I am — not just to my friends but also to my community. It doesn't matter where we've come from, or what our unique "fun fact" may be; what matters is the journey we take to get to our destinations, and the lessons we learn along the way.

My message from the mess is to be gentle with myself. I even welcome the messes now. Without them, the growth in my life would not have happened as it has. I've not only learned valuable lessons from my messes, but they've also taught me to be gentler and more patient with others. I can proceed with grace when I see other people going through messes of their own. Letting go of the fear of judgment has truly given me an abundant life that I fully and happily embrace each day.

The mess: Living a life controlled by the fear of judgment.

The message: Letting go of the fear of judgment allows me to live fully and to open myself up to new and amazing friendships.

Action step: Start a judgment journal. Become aware of how judgment shows up in your life – jot down when you feel you are being judged or if you catch yourself unfairly judging another person. Work on changing any unhealthy patterns that you notice.

Journal

Todays date is:

This book has changed my life in the following ways:

"We will always be friends till we are old and senile. Then we can be new friends."

— Anonymous

Going Forward

These conversations with my friends changed — and continue to change — my life. Taking the Mess-to-Message Challenge via virtual dates during the COVID-19 pandemic stay-at-home orders helped pull me through the isolation that I felt as the days turned into weeks, the weeks turned into months, and the months ultimately added up to over one solid year of social distancing.

I learned that we all have messes. Even among close friends, there are daily messes that we experience that we don't share with one another. For example, it surprised me to learn how many of my friends struggle daily with anxiety and depression. Learning this gave me an even greater gratitude for the effort it takes for them to show up as they do. It also made me realize that I need to listen more carefully to my friends, ask questions, and simply check in — to be present as a friend.

Following these dates, in my work as a life coach, I now regularly encourage my clients to explore the possible messages that are in their messes. And now it's your turn:

What is the mess that became your message?

I hope you'll not only answer that question for yourself but also choose to take the challenge! Let's look at it one more time:

The Challenge:
Over the course of a year, commit to meet with at least three people, one on one:

1. **A life-long friend**
2. **A relative**
3. **A new acquaintance or someone you've known for a while but have never shared a meal with**

And ask the question, "What is the mess that became your message?"

Document your dates on social media with the hashtag #messtomessagechallenge

Let's learn, grow, and journey together!

Contact Us

An Imperfectly Perfect Life
PO Box 592
Redmond, WA 98073
tel. 206-225-7643
www.animperfectlyperfectlife.com

Let's get social:
https://www.facebook.com/animperfectlyperfectlife
https://www.instagram.com/an_imperfectly_perfect_life/
https://www.linkedin.com/in/shari-leid-51a53b10/
https://twitter.com/AnImperfectly

Please visit www.animperfectlyperfectlife.com to view video interviews with the women that you just read about and to sign up to receive exclusive offers, including a free mindset strategy coaching session and downloadable tools that you can use to turn your mess into your amazing message!